T0149067

A Silent Action

A Silent Action:
Engagements with
Thomas Merton

Rowan Williams

FONS VITAE

First published in 2011 by
Fons Vitae
49 Mockingbird Valley Drive
Louisville, KY 40207
http://www.fonsvitae.com
Email: fonsvitaeky@aol.com

Library of Congress Control Number: 2011934726
ISBN 9781891785788

Printed in Canada

For their invaluable help, gratitude is extended to Brother Patrick Hart,
Brother Paul Quenon, Anne Ogden, Gray Zeitz, Jonathan Greene,
Maryam Faugnos, and Diane and Christopher Meatyard, and for their
generous support, to:

Reverend Alfred Shands

Lady Susan Jennifer Hunt	Janey Newton
Babs Hardy	Mary Clay Stites
John, Ginny, and Woo Speed	Jane and Paul Jones
Cissy Musselman	Sandra and Buddy Thompson
Lindy and Bill Street	Nana Lampton
Edith S. Bingham	Emily Bingham and Stephen Reily
Nina and Ned Bonnie	Jill Cooper
Cynthia and Bob Greene	Eleanor Bingham Miller
Alice Gray and Walker Stites	Christy and Owsley Brown
Laura Lee Lyons Brown	Gray Henry and Neville Blakemore

For Mary

Table of Contents

Illustrations

Ordination Day: Photograph of Thomas Merton. Used with permission of the Merton Legacy Trust and the Thomas Merton Center, Bellarmine University. Louisville, Kentucky.

Saint John Chrysostom: The State Tretyakov Gallery, Andrei Rublev Gallery, Moscow.

Thomas Merton: Used with permission of the Estate of Ralph Eugene Meatyard.

Hagia Sophia: Woodcut by Victor Hammer with permission from Gay Reading and Dr. Paul Holbrook, The King Library Press, University of Kentucky, Lexington, Kentucky.

Karl Barth: Karl Barth Archiv, Basel; photographed by Maria Netter, December, 1955.

The Old Choir at the Abbey of Gethsemani: from the archives at the Abbey of Gethsemani, Trappist, Kentucky.

Author's Foreword

I began reading Thomas Merton as a teenager, wrestling with *The Sign of Jonas* more than once, fascinated by the richness of the writing, attracted by the intensity of the spiritual energy; and then, when I read *Elected Silence*, the abridged British edition of *The Seven Storey Mountain*, I began to understand more of the human complexity of the man. As I've said in one of the chapters in this little book, *Conjectures of a Guilty Bystander* came my way when I was first studying theology and had a transfiguring impact, drawing together themes and writers I already knew and loved in a fresh vision and linking them with the global questions about war and poverty that I was beginning, like so many of my generation, to see as inseparable from taking contemplation and sacraments seriously. And studying for my doctorate with Merton's friend A.M. Allchin, proved a doorway into still more of his mind and spirit; the longest chapter in this book represents some of the thinking I was doing in conversation with Donald Allchin during those years. A few years later, the *Asian Journal* gave me my first sense that inter-religious dialogue could be (and had to be) a matter of spiritual encounter, and still more doors opened.

Most of Merton's readers will have been tempted to echo the words of his delightful teenage correspondent, Suzanne Butorovich—'GOOD GRIEF, why do you write so much?' And the first piece in the present book reflects both an unease with and a way of making sense of Merton's compulsive need to try out—or perhaps try on—the latest idioms and perspectives he has encountered in his reading. What the published journals document at length is the way in which this chameleon-like dimension to his mind was always being abraded and refined by a sharply self-critical honesty. Repeatedly, when you are inclined to exasperation at Merton's ability to dramatise himself in yet another set of borrowed clothes, you are brought up short by his own clear-eyed acknowledgement that this is what he is doing. Like many great religious poets and autobiographers, he uses his writing, private and public, to exorcise rather than indulge fantasy. And, as the last chapter here underlines, he discovers more and more deeply the serious unseriousness of trying to be honest before God—the 'unbearable lightness' of faith. I believe this is by no means the least important thing he brings to his readers, especially at a season of humourless anxiety in so much of the life of historic Christianity.

This book comprises a number of 'engagements' with Merton over nearly forty years; but what has rather surprised me in reading them over is the continuity of the concerns. Going back repeatedly to Merton has felt like picking up an interrupted conversation, and I have recognised how much the stimulus of his writing has been an unbroken element in my own life and thinking. In revising these pieces for republication, I have added some passages to draw out the continuities, to reinforce the fact that once you have begun to engage with Merton, seeds are sown for long thoughts and prayers—seeds of contemplation, you might say; he is not someone who is read once and then filed away. Putting together these pieces has given me a welcome opportunity of expressing an enormous debt of gratitude to a writer who for so many has changed the landscape of Christian reflection once and for all, and enriched generations of men and women willing to think and to pray with him.

I must also pay the warmest of tributes to Gray Henry, who so generously proposed the idea of this book, and to Jonathan and Sarah Goodall for invaluable help in assembling, transcribing, and editing the material.

Rowan Williams
Lambeth Palace, London
Advent 2010

Preface

It is a pity Thomas Merton and Rowan Williams never met. What a friendship it would have been. Their age difference was the obstacle—Rowan was only eighteen when Merton died. Yet there is another sense in which meetings occur and friendships spring to life despite the impossibility of correspondence or face-to-face encounter. Good writing always remains in the present tense; the attentive reader meets the author in the intimate space of the printed page. When that occurs, a relationship can take root that flourishes despite the problem of death.

One sees the reality of such a friendship in this slim volume that brings together Rowan's explorations of Merton's writings. Merton would have been delighted to have found himself so carefully and perceptively read. The correspondence between them would have made this a much larger book.

In fact Merton's own life, especially once he had become a monk, was to a great extent one of dialogue with people who were either distant or dead (many saints and writers of past centuries).

Rowan looks closely at two such relationships in Merton's life—first with the Orthodox theologian, Paul Evdokimov, and then with Karl Barth, the Reformed theologian who, by a surprising providence, died on the same day as Merton. Rowan also takes note of the impact on Merton's thought of books by Hannah Arendt, Dostoevsky, Vladimir Lossky, Olivier Clément, Bonhoeffer, Boris Pasternak, and St. John of the Cross.

Not the least of the many meeting points for Merton and Rowan is their Orwell-like awareness of the abuse of language, so easily used for magical (that is to say, manipulative) ends. Thus war is described and justified in words that mask its actual purposes, dehumanize the adversary, and cloak its actual cost in human agony. The problem extends to religious words as well—ways of speaking about God that flatten rather than unveil. 'Words of faith,' Rowan observes, 'are too-well known to believers for their meaning to be knowable.' Indeed, 'almost any words in the modern cultural setting will be worn and shabby or illusory and self-serving.' Rowan sees in Merton's writings how, with ascetic effort, language can be restored to the transparent state of plain speech, a revealer of truth, a preserver of freedom, but this involves a day-by-day, word-by-word, sentence-by-sentence struggle.

We see in these several essays that Rowan, no less than Merton, regards Christian life without a contemplative dimension as incomplete and also recognizes that the contemplative life is accessible not only to those living in monasteries but to anyone who seeks an 'interiorized' monasticism, for 'contemplative prayer is the vocation of every believer.' One of the major tasks of contemplative life is the ongoing search for the actual self, the unmasked self, a self that is not merely the stage clothes and scripted sentences that we assemble and dutifully exhibit each day in the attempt to appear to be someone, but the self that exists purely because it exists in God. Rowan notes how often Merton is drawn to a 'delusory self image' but then quickly abandons each self-image as a ridiculous deception.

Merton's pilgrimage, from his initial attraction to the Trappists until the day of his death, was to disappear—that is not to be the brand name 'Thomas Merton' or a Thomas Merton who has become mainly the bearer of various labels: monk, writer, contemplative, mystic, etc. Twice in this book Rowan cites a passage from *The Sign of Jonas* that he first read when he was eighteen: 'I have to be a person that nobody knows. They can have Thomas Merton. He's dead. Father Louis—he's half-dead too.' In fact, for all Merton's grumbling about his famous adversary, Thomas Merton, he remained Thomas Merton, fully alive and always writing in a voice that was intensely and recognizably his own—but a Merton who was unwilling to make himself the prisoner of his readers' expectations and illusions. (No doubt the struggle not to be defined purely by an ecclesiastical role is every bit as pressing to Rowan as it was to Merton.) 'Truth can only be spoken by a man nobody knows,' Rowan writes, 'because only in the unknown person is there no obstruction to reality: the ego of self-oriented desire and manifold qualities, seeking to dominate and organize the world, is absent.'

Both Merton and Rowan are people who have drawn deeply from Eastern Christian sources, both ancient and modern. Rowan's doctoral dissertation concentrated on the work of Vladimir Lossky, whose writings also had great impact on Merton. Lossky was one of the Paris-based Orthodox theologians who distinguished the 'individual' from the 'person,' the latter understood as the self existing in communion with others rather than attempting to live in a state of one-person *apartheid*. To the extent one is becoming a person,

Rowan notes, the process of sanctity is underway, for one 'cannot be simply an individual pursuing an impossible ideal of individual sanctification in a sort of spiritual solipsism; this is, rather, the condition characteristic of hell.'

For the Orthodox Christian, it is often noted, there are 'at least' seven sacraments. On the long list that can be attached to the seven, surely one is the mystery of friendship: an enduring relationship held together not only by affinity, shared questions and common interests, but the awareness that each can help the other in a quest—a partnership in pilgrimage. As the bond between Rowan Williams and Thomas Merton bears witness, not all friendships depend on being of the same generation or even being simultaneously alive.

Jim Forest
December 8, 2010

Acknowledgements

All the pieces in this collection have been previously published:

Chapter 1

"'A person that nobody knows': a paradoxical tribute to Thomas Merton" appeared in *Cistercian Studies*, xiii (1978), 399–401, and was reprinted in the *Merton Journal*, 9.2 (Advent 2002), pp.46–47.

Chapter 2

"'Bread in the Wilderness': the monastic ideal in Thomas Merton and Paul Evdokimov" originally appeared in A. M. Allchin, ed.: *Theology and Prayer: essays on monastic themes presented to the Oxford Cistercian Conference, 1973* (Oxford, 1975) and in *One Yet Two: Monastic Traditions in East and West*, Cistercian Studies 29 (1976), pp.452–73; reprinted in J. Montaldo: *Merton and Hesychasm: the prayer of the heart* (Louisville KY, 2003), pp.175–96.

Chapter 3

"'New Words for God': contemplation and religious writing," in P. M. Pearson et al: *Thomas Merton: poet, monk, prophet* (Abergavenny: Three Peaks Press, 1998), pp.39–47.

Chapter 4

"'The Only Real City': monasticism and the social vision" was given as an address at a Merton Conference at the Monastery of Bose, 2004, and was published as "'The Courage not to Abstain from Speaking": Monasticism, Culture and the Modern World in the public interventions of a Disturbing Monk' in *Merton Journal*, xii/1 (2005), pp.8–18.

Chapter 5

"'Not Being Serious': Thomas Merton and Karl Barth" in *Merton Journal*, 16.2 (Advent 2009), pp.14–22; lecture given on 10 December 2008 to the UK Thomas Merton Society (at St. Cyprian's, Clarence Gate, London) on the occasion of the fortieth anniversary of Merton's death in 1968.

Poem

"Thomas Merton: summer 1966" in *The Poems of Rowan Williams* (Oxford: Perpetua Press and Grand Rapids: Erdmanns, 2002), p.49.

Chapter 1
'A person that nobody knows':
A Paradoxical Tribute to Thomas Merton

"Truth can only be spoken by a man nobody knows, because only in the *unknown* person is there no obstruction to reality: the ego of self-oriented desire and manifold qualities, seeking to dominate and organize the world, is absent. There is no one there to know . . . " (*See* p.17)

Chapter 1
'A person that nobody knows':
A Paradoxical Tribute to Thomas Merton

'I have to be a person that nobody knows. They can have Thomas Merton. He's dead. Father Louis—he's half-dead too.'[1] He must, even as he wrote those angular words, have been well aware of their irony; and now, more than forty years after his death, they are odder than ever. 'He's dead': but 'Thomas Merton' is one of the most wearisomely familiar names in the canon of modern spiritual writing, and the whole industry of Merton Studies has blossomed (if that is the word) and shows no sign of diminution. Indeed, I am busily contributing to it as I write these words.

He was, however, quite right. We 'have' Thomas Merton, and the Thomas Merton we have, who is the subject of Merton Studies, *is* dead, dead and in no small danger of becoming dull. Merton's own anarchic sense of the absurd would have found wry satisfaction in the uncritical reverence accorded to his most ephemeral utterances; and I do not think he would have been best pleased at the sight of an illustrated new edition of *The Seven Storey Mountain,* when he had gone to such pains in his later years to insist that it was, for him, an historical document—that he had, curiously and humanly enough, changed his mind. We are determined that we *shall* know him, in all the meticulous detail possible. And so (because providence too has a vengeful irony) we shall make it quite, quite certain that he will indeed be 'a person that nobody knows.' As unknown and yet well-known.[2]

What we are in danger of forgetting is something utterly fundamental to Merton, something which makes more intelligible the fact that he could give almost equal veneration to Catholic and Buddhist traditions. It is the theme of the illusory self. Truth can only be spoken by a man nobody knows, because only in the *unknown* person is there no obstruction to reality: the ego of self-oriented desire and manifold qualities, seeking to dominate and organize the world, is absent. There is no-one there to know; but what *is* there to know is the form, the configuration of a wider reality expressed in one place,

17

one story. It will not be the story of an interesting and original personality, but the story of one series of responses to and reflections of the currents and structures of the world.

Merton did not believe that the concrete and the historical were unimportant; no Christian could seriously so believe, and to put it in those crude terms does not do justice to the Oriental perspective either. But he did believe that truth was found not in the pursuit of an individual fulfilment or destiny, but in responsive attention to every possible human (concrete and historical) influence. There is no isolated, pure, and independent 'I,' but there is a vast and universal web of 'I's, in which I have a true and right place. And understanding for me and for you comes by concentration not on your or my ego as such, but upon the web, the interrelation, through and in its several component points. This is—clumsily put—an aspect of the characteristic Eastern understanding of *dharma*. In the *Asian Journal*,[3] Merton quotes the Hindu writer, G. B. Mohan, on the function of poetry—'to make us aware of this dharma'—and the nature of the poetic enterprise as allowing an 'insight into the complexities of our moral existence' by 'recreating another's experience in our self.' And Merton sees this as especially true of 'anti-poetry,' and concrete poetry, in which poetic meaning is found simply in the ironic reply of routine and banal meanings in another voice.[4] Clearly this becomes possible only by a kind of withdrawing of the ego from poetry, so that the poetic voice is little more than a sounding board. And here again we return to the need for truth to be sought in selfless attentiveness—'this listening, this questioning, this humble and courageous exposure to what the world ignores about itself[5]—in responsiveness to *dharma*.'

This is a Christian view, not only because the gospels too preach the renunciation of self, but because Christian belief finds the ground of truth in the silence of Christ, in the story of a man so 'poor' that, at the end of his days, he preaches no word, no idea, but suffers only, takes the world to himself by resisting nothing of it, by exercising none of the self's habitual violence, and whose life is thus transparent without qualification to the shape of reality. A man nobody knows. The distinctive Christian way is to find the grace of selfless, compassionate existence by attention to and identification with the unique and unrepeatable *total* instance of it within the net of *dharma*. And thus the priest or monk whose calling it is to guide, nurture, and, in some manner, act out this way must see himself

Christologically, as Merton so eminently did, writing of the 'poverty' of the priest who 'vanishes into the Mass.'[6]

Into the Mass, and into the whole world which is gathered into it. Merton's genius was largely that he was a massively unoriginal man: he is extraordinary because he is so dramatically absorbed by every environment he finds himself in—America between the wars, classical pre-conciliar Catholicism and monasticism, the peace movement, Asia. In all these contexts he is utterly 'priestly' because utterly *attentive*: he does not organize, dominate, or even interpret, much of the time, but responds. It is not a chameleon inconsistency (though it could be so interpreted by a hostile eye), because all these influences flow in to one constant place, a will and imagination turned Godward. Merton is sure enough of his real place, his real roots, to let some very strange and very strong winds blow over him, to let his understanding grow by this constant re-creation in himself of other human possibilities. And so, in the long run, being interested in Thomas Merton is *not* being interested in an original, a 'shaping' mind, but being interested in God and human possibilities. Merton will not *let* me look at him for long: he will, finally, persuade me to look in the direction he is looking. That is one reason why this is a short article. I don't want to know much more about Merton; he is dead, and I shall commend him regularly, lovingly, and thankfully to God. I am concerned to find how I can turn further in the direction he is looking, in prayer, poetry, theology, and encounter with the experience of other faiths; in trust and love of God our saviour.

The great Christian is the man or woman who can make me more interested in God than in him or her. A paradoxical tribute, but the highest that can be paid.

Chapter 2
'Bread in the Wilderness':
The Monastic Ideal in Thomas Merton
and Paul Evdokimov

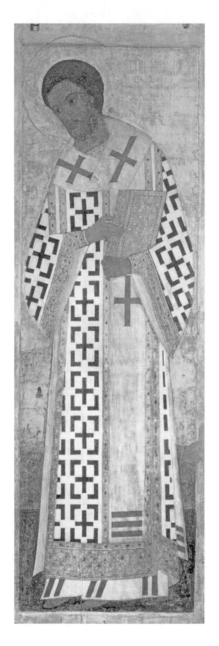

' . . . the saint is an "icon" not merely in the sense that he "stands for"
or "witnesses to" the divine order, but because he is truly the channel
through which God's energies enter into the human world. The saint's
vision of the world is *God's* vision of the world, because the saint is
'transparent' to God: in the person of the saint contemplating God,
God contemplates the world.' (*See* p. 34)

Chapter 2
'Bread in the Wilderness':
The Monastic Ideal in Thomas Merton
and Paul Evdokimov

Many readers of Merton have probably acquired their only knowledge of the thought of Paul Evdokimov through a long passage in
Conjectures of a Guilty Bystander[1] in which Merton (mistakenly
assuming, by the way, that Evdokimov was a priest) discusses Evdokimov's vision of a 'radical tradition of monasticism, both Eastern
and Western.' It is an impressively sympathetic discussion; Evdokimov's ideal clearly answers to a very great amount in Merton's own
thought, already developing with increasing reference to the Eastern
tradition in general, and the Desert Fathers in particular. What I
hope to do in this essay is to investigate some of the more interesting
points of convergence between these two theologians, and thereby
to explore a little of what this 'radical tradition' implies.

Certainly, one of the most significant aspects of such a convergence is that it appears in two thinkers who are at once profoundly
rooted in their own traditions and genuinely open to others: Merton's spirituality owes its fundamental orientation to the Cistercian
and Carmelite traditions, and, as Evelyn Waugh rightly indicated,[2] to
French Catholicism, but it would not be what it is without his devoted
and careful study of Greek patristic thought and the Desert Fathers.
Evdokimov, a Russian emigré who spent his entire working life in
France, is essentially a product of the Russian religio-philosophical
and literary ethos of Gogol and Dostoevsky, Florensky, Bulgakov,
and Berdyaev, an ethos itself very much aware of the spirituality of
the 'desert' which was to become so central to Evdokimov's theology. Yet his understanding of French religious and anti-religious
culture, from Bloy and Claudel to Sartre, is remarkable. What we
are witnessing is a rapprochement not merely between the 'monastic culture' (to borrow Merton's own term[3]) of Roman Catholicism
and that of Orthodoxy, but between distinct 'religious cultures,' in a
wider sense; and the interest in Kierkegaard shared by Merton and
Evdokimov suggests the possibility of a further convergence, with

a particular strand in another 'religious culture,' that of Continental Lutheranism. That, however, is a subject which would require another paper to itself.

It is Evdokimov's treatment of the question of *authenticity* which seems to interest Merton most in the discussion to which I have referred: 'one goes into the desert to vomit up the interior phantom, the doubter, the double'[4] is Evdokimov's phrase, and Merton, as we might expect, responds enthusiastically to the idea of asceticism as 'therapy,' humanizing therapy, implicit in this formulation. The preoccupation with authenticity is, I think, one of the most consistent unifying themes traceable in Merton's work, from the time of *Elected Silence* onwards; indeed, even further back, in the *Secular Journal*, which contains material written between 1939 and 1941, we find a succession of wryly humorous dialogues with a sceptical interlocutor, in which questions of personal and artistic integrity are obviously much to the fore in Merton's mind.[5] Here, too, we find one of the only two explicit allusions in the *Journal* to Merton's painful decision to risk being refused entry to the Franciscan novitiate in 1940.[6]

However, the superb passage on Kierkegaard and the 'teleological suspension of ethics'[7] is a moving and revealing commentary on the insights gained through this decision, which was, as *Elected Silence* makes clear, very definitely prompted by considerations of 'authenticity.' Of his anticipations of life as a friar, Merton dryly comments that 'it made a pleasant picture.'[8] It represented an attempt to create a new existence essentially divorced from the reality of his previous life, with no attempt at a healing or integration of that previous life; a new existence, therefore, which could not be other than artificial, *inauthentic*. At the same time, his attraction to the Franciscan life is recognized as being no more than a translation into vocational terms of a set of inclinations and attractions purely natural in character, 'investing the future with all kinds of natural pleasures and satisfactions which would fortify and defend my ego against the troubles and worries of life in the world.'[9] There is no *metanoia* here; any illusion that there is, is based upon the superficial divorce from, and suppression of, a 'sinful' past. It is not difficult to misrepresent this section of *Elected Silence;* Merton's expressions are often obscure, and can be read as suggesting

24

merely a kind of tormented scrupulosity, a moralistic awareness of 'unworthiness' for the religious life. To some extent, indeed, it *is* a moralistic vocabulary which he uses here, and a rather conventional language of 'renunciation of natural goods'; but I hope I have shown some reason for seeing his decision as, fundamentally, concerned with a crisis of 'integrity.' There is here, surely, an implicit recognition that the monastic vocation demands a real encounter with one's own 'nothingness,' with the false and illusory *persona* created by one's betrayal of the true self, the image of God, in a concordat with a false and illusory society.

At this point, we may turn to examine Evdokimov's explanation of the rise of monasticism; and it is precisely the 'concordat' with society and history which Evdokimov sees as driving the monk into the desert: *'Après le concordat qui installait l'Église dans l'histoire et lui offrait son statut légal et une existence paisible, le témoignage que les martyrs rendaient aux choses denières passe au monachisme et s'y transforme en ministère du maximalisme eschatologique.'*[10] ['After the concordat that had established the Church in history and offered it its legal status and a peaceful existence, the testimony borne by the martyrs concerning the last things passed over into monasticism and was transformed there into a mystery of ultimate eschatological commitment.'] 'For "those who love his coming," the Christian city that the Empire of Constantine undertook to build is profoundly ambiguous.'[11] What the monk is doing is witnessing to a radical eschatological *folly* in the midst of a church which has learned to sit lightly to the apocalyptic violence of the gospel, to pitch its tent in history, to allow itself to be *defined* by history and by the present *saeculum*. Monasticism is a provisional phenomenon,[12] existing for as long as the Church exists as a function of the city, the state, until the city is truly baptised. Not only Kierkegaard on 'Christendom,' but Dostoevsky on Church and state is echoed here: 'It is not the Church that ought to be turned into a State, as from a lower to a higher form, but, on the contrary, the State ought to end by being worthy to become only the Church and nothing else.'[13] The Church has failed to recognize the devils in the city, and so the monk seeks them out in the desert; the only real reason for the flight to the desert is this impulse to confront the diabolical, the infernal, which threatens all men, be they ever so oblivious of it.

In other words, in the more familiar terminology of twentieth-century existentialism, the monk recoils in horror, anguish, and nausea from the possibilities of 'bad faith' which life in the city presents to him and other men.[14] The monk is called to face the threat of nothingness, whether in 'bad faith' or in the constant awareness of finitude and death, without any of the anodynes provided by life in society: *'Les athlètes de l'ascèse pouvaient se mesurer avec les démons, car seuls ils étaient capables de les voir face à face et de supporter cette vision redoutable (les ascètes parlent de la puanteur insupportable des démons, de la "nausée de l'esprit" qu'ils provoquent).'*[15] ['The athletes of ascesis could take on demons, for they alone were capable of beholding them face-to-face and bearing this fearful sight (the ascetics mention the unbearable stench of the demons, the "nausea of the spirit" they provoke).'] The monk's service to the city he leaves is the objectification of its demons, so that they become visible and identifiable for men; his immense risk, his total exposure of himself, has a universal 'therapeutic' effect,[16] redeeming the Church, and thus, finally, the world, from bondage to blindness and untruth, from submission to the false, 'demoniacal' self-image (individual or collective) which is not recognised until it is 'personalized' in the solitary combat of the ascetic with the devils in the wilderness.

'This is precisely the monk's chief service to the world: this silence, this listening, this questioning, this humble and courageous exposure to what the world ignores about itself—*both good and evil.*'[17] The going-out of the monk into the desert is a sign of hope to the city as well as a sign of judgement, because it testifies to our ability to face and to reject illusion; it is an act performed in imitation of Christ, partaking in the salvific quality of his temptation in the wilderness. Evdokimov rightly reminds us of the great significance attached by many of the Greek Fathers (especially Justin, Irenaeus, and Origen) to the temptations of Christ in the economy of salvation, the *anakephalaiosis* of human existence and the realisation of the image of God in us;[18] it is the reversal of the consequences of Adam's defeat by the tempter, and thus the opening to us of the new possibility of victory over falsehood and inauthenticity. Christ in the desert prepares the way for the Christian in the desert. Evdokimov's particular use of the temptation narratives is, predictably, very much influenced by the brilliant analysis of the three temptations in Dostoevsky's parable of the Grand Inquisitor, as temptations to the exercise of 'miracle, mystery, and authority.'[19] 'Satan advances three infallible solutions of human destiny: the alchemist *miracle* of the philosopher's stone, the *mystery* of occult sciences and their boundless powers; and finally one unifying *authority*.'[20] In these temptations is summed up the whole of the diabolical invitation to falsehood and 'nothingness,' that 'self-destruction and non-existence'[21] of which Satan is the personification. And these are the temptations which the Empire offered to the Church, and to which the Church, or, at least, the greater part of it, has succumbed, according to Dostoevsky and Evdokimov.

Thus we can see how the monk's rejection of the city is grounded in Christ's victory over the temptor: 'If the empire made its secret temptation out of Satan's three invitations, monasticism was openly built on Christ's three immortal answers.'[22] We should, Evdokimov suggests, see the three traditional vows of the religious state as corresponding precisely to Christ's three replies to Satan. The refusal to turn stones into bread corresponds to the vow of *poverty:* it is 'the primacy ... of grace over necessity,'[23] the rejection of a scale of values in which the material satisfaction associated with property is considered self-evidently good. The poor man, the monk who possesses nothing, can share nothing but 'his *being,* his eucharistic flesh and blood,'[24] and is free to be the brother of all. The refusal of Jesus to cast himself from the pinnacle of the temple corresponds to the vow of *chastity:* it is the 'purification of the heart' in love and reverence towards the whole of creation, the refusal of a certain kind of 'power' over the cosmos, a power which is a mockery, an abuse and an exploitation of the place which God gives to humanity in the world. The monk's chastity is an 'integration' of his human powers over matter in a new attitude of what Simone Weil would call 'attention' to created things. Evdokimov points to the mysterious relationship between woman and the cosmos apprehended in so many of the mystery cults of pre-Christian Europe and Asia, and discernible even in the cult of the Mother of God.[25] Continence towards woman and reverence for creation are intimately connected. Finally, Jesus' refusal to bow down and worship Satan corresponds to the vow of *obedience:* the refusal of slavery to Satan, to illusion and falsehood, is liberation into obedience to him 'whose service is perfect freedom.' Evdokimov quotes from the *Apophthegmata Patrum* to illustrate his contention that monastic obedience is fundamentally different from the secular model of submission to authority: 'Never command, but be for all an example, never a lawgiver';[26] 'I shall say nothing. Do, if you want, what you see me do';[27] 'Every counsel of a *starets* (elder, spiritual father) leads a man to a state of freedom before the face of God.'[28]

Merton nowhere (to my knowledge) develops such a close analogy between Our Lord's temptations and the vows of the religious state; but I hope it will become clear that the monastic ideal outlined by Evdokimov is very close indeed to Merton's own. Certainly the type of religious obedience which Evdokimov speaks of is precisely what Merton finds so impressive in the *Apophthegmata:* obedience preserves the monk from the dangers of being a law to himself, of persevering in the falsehood of self-will and self-love which he has fled the city to escape. 'His search in the desert is not merely for solitude in which he can simply do as he pleases and admire himself as a great contemplative. There would be no real quiet in such an exploit, or, if there were peace, it would be the false peace of self-assurance and self-complacency.'[29] Obedience is a necessary concomitant of *metanoia*, delivery from the worship of the illusory ego; and this, of course, is as much as to say that the mere fact of geographical separation from the city, from society, does not of itself deliver the monk from illusion. What the monastic tradition calls 'compunction' (πενθος) and Merton, following the existentialists, calls 'dread,' is a constantly recurring experience in the monastic life.[30]

There is a danger of a wrong sort of objectification of the diabolical, of refusing to recognise its radical presence in *oneself,* and its persistence within oneself, even when the appropriate gestures of renunciation have been made. It is perhaps the new awareness of this that lies underneath the tormented questionings of Part Five of *The Sign of Jonas,* the discovery that a new and more subtle temptation to falsehood and unreality awaits the monk in his community, that it is as easy to yield to the imposition of an illusory definition of the self by the purely external observance of the religious community as to submit to the definition of the self offered by society. It is revealing to look at (what seems to me to be) a climacteric passage in this section of *The Sign of Jonas:* 'In order to be not remembered or wanted I have to be a person that nobody knows. They can have Thomas Merton. He's dead. Father Louis—he's half-dead too.'[31]

The true solitude in which the monk must face his nothingness is to be found, finally, only in the monk himself: 'Even though he may live in a community, the monk is bound to explore the inner waste of his own being as a solitary.'[32] And in the opening essay of *Raids on the Unspeakable,* one of the places in which he explicitly makes use of the temptation narratives of the Gospels, Merton quotes, from the sixth-century Syrian ascetic, Philoxenos, a passage on the monk following Christ into the desert 'to fight the power of error,' and comments: 'And where is the power of error? We find it was after all not in the city, but in *ourselves.*'[33]

The 'geographical' desert, then, is adjectival to the true personal solitude of the monk, and to think otherwise is to refuse to see that the flight of the first monks to the desert, although a protest against compromise with history, was itself an *historical* phenomenon, a particular manifestation in a particular period of history: 'Certainly *now* there can be no possible return to the desert. We are in different times and above all in different *spiritual ages.*'[34] Indeed, Evdokimov suggests that the Fathers of the Desert have paved the way for a return to history, to the city, to society; once the reality of the interior desert has been seen, in the city and in the wilderness, the resultant deep transformation of the human consciousness becomes, to a greater or lesser degree, independent of external circumstances. 'Human consciousness was different before the ascesis of the desert from what it was after. Just like the event of Pentecost, this ascesis has modified the dominant energies of the psyche and has renewed the human spirit.'[35] The extremism, the 'eschatological maximalism' of the desert, is a necessary dialectical step in the development of the Christian consciousness toward a position of equilibrium; and because, in the present world order, we cannot hope ever to attain and preserve such a position, the monk's physical or geographical separation from society remains an indispensable witness.

However, it is now possible for the monastic state to exist as 'interiorised' in the layperson: and Evdokimov supports his plea for 'interiorised monasticism' with an impressive array of quotations from Chrysostom, Theodore of Studium, and others on the essential unity of all Christian spirituality, whether practiced by priest, monk, or layperson. The monastic experience of exposure to the diabolical possibilities inherent in human existence, especially Christian existence in 'the world,' and the monastic reiteration of Christ's refusal of Satan's temptations are part of the vocation of every believer. What they imply, finally, is a condition of receptivity to the Holy Spirit, the Spirit of Truth, who is alike the giver and the gift of authentic human being. Monasticism is a universal *epiclesis,* an invocation of the Spirit upon all humanity and all creation;[36] there must be no weakening of its demands by any such evasion as the traditional distinction between 'counsel' and 'precept' in the Gospel. The encounter of the monk with God is the same encounter to which all Christians are called; and here, of course, we are reminded of Merton's constant insistence that contemplative prayer is the vocation of every believer,[37] or, rather, that the 'contemplative dimension' (for lack of a better expression) exists in everyone, and that the Christian is called upon to realise it as their true identity, their *'identity-in-God.'* 'Discovering the contemplative life is a new self discovery. One might say it is the flowering of a deeper identity on an entirely different plane from a mere psychological discovery, a paradoxical new identity that is found only in loss of self.'[38] This is not the place for a detailed discussion of the central importance for Merton of the doctrine of humanity as the image of God (for such a discussion, I would commend in particular the first two chapters of Higgins' study), but it should be noted that this explanation of contemplative prayer implies that confrontation with, or awakening to, the true self is awakening to God; so that the condition of inauthenticity, falsehood, clinging to the illusory self-image precludes any real encounter with God.

Noverim Me Noverim Te; to know God in this 'coming to ourselves' is to know ourselves as God knows us, to know our true identity. The 'opposition' between us and God is done away with, and we may speak of our 'divinisation,' 'the ultimate in man's self-realisation.'[39] To arrive at 'true identity' is to arrive at true *personhood,* since one is 'not a person in the fullest spiritual sense of the word'[40] if one does not yet truly know oneself. 'We must long to learn the secret of our own nothingness (not God's secret first of all, but our own secret). But God alone can show us our own secret.'[41] If every person's identity is hidden in God, every person's bound to seek it through that perilous exposure to God in solitude which is the basis of contemplation. Contemplation is not a religious exercise but an ontological necessity in the intense *personalism* of Christian faith, the encounter of the human person with the Divine Council of Persons.

Evdokimov likewise reiterates the profound identity of the mystery of God and the mystery of humanity: *'Le mystère du Createur vient se refléter dans le miroir de la créature et fait dire à Théophile d'Antioche: "Montre-moi ton homme, et je te montrerai mon Dieu." Saint Pierre parle de l'homocordis absconditus, l'homme caché du coeur. (I P 3:4). Le Deus absconditus, Dieu mystérieux, a créé son vis-à-vis: l'homo absconditus, l'homme mystérieux, son icone vivant.'* [42] ['The mystery of the Creator is reflected in the mirror of the creature and makes Theophilus of Antioch say: "Show me your human being and I shall show you my God." Saint Peter speaks of the *homo cordis absconditus*, the hidden man of the heart. The *Deus absconditus*, the mysterious God, has created his counterpart: the *homo absconditus*, the mysterious man, his living image.'] All human beings have the potential for true personhood, because all have the capacity for self-awareness, which Evdokimov designates as the property of the *prosōpon*; it is when this self-awareness is perfected in communion with God, in the realization of the image of God, that the human individual becomes *hupostasis*, a person whose personhood is analogous to that of the Persons of the Trinity. The *prosōpon* alone can become trapped in individuality, whereas the *hupostasis* exists in a state of communion with other persons. [43]

Thus, if the monk, the solitary, is engaged in the process of becoming a *person,* he cannot be simply an individual pursuing an impossible ideal of individual sanctification in a sort of spiritual solipsism; this is, rather, the condition characteristic of hell. [44] The spirit of man at its deepest level is 'intentional,' turned toward the other; [45] and again we may say that a denial of this intentionality with regard to other persons and to the world in general prevents us from ever realizing our position as partners in dialogue with God. 'We can never keep ourselves alone before God; we are saved only together, 'collegially,' as Soloviev said: *"he will be saved who saves others."'* [46] The purpose of the ascetic life is the attainment of 'a heart inflamed with charity for the entire creation,' [47] in the words of Isaac of Nineveh which Evdokimov was so fond of quoting. The Christian is baptized into the death of Christ, into his descent to hell, into a condition of *vulnerability* to the suffering of the whole of humanity; so that the solitary who goes out to face the demons is exploring the consequences of his baptism, his being-in-Christ. [48] Paradoxically, his calling to be alone with Christ in the desert is made possible by his existence in the

Church, in 'communion,' because it is thus that he becomes sensitive and vulnerable to the presence of the demons afflicting mankind; in the desert he has to bear the weight not only of his own interior devils, but of the world's suffering and bondage. The solitary is such because he is a member of Christ's body, and so, ultimately, because he is a human being: and his way must, in some measure, be the way of all members of Christ's body, and so of all human beings.

Solitude, then, is a form of *kenosis*: the solitary is not merely imitating a past event when he follows Christ into the desert, he is *participating* in the whole work of Christ, the *kenosis* of the whole of his existence as 'the lamb slain from the foundation of the world.' We have already seen, in the first part of this essay, how the life of the monk is grounded in Christ's 'recapitulation' of human nature, his perfect realization of the divine image in us; now we may understand also that, just as this restoration of humanity is only achieved by the eternal self-emptying of the Word made flesh, so the monk's refusal of falsehood and his commitment to the search for 'authenticity' are made possible only by his baptism into the death of Christ, his sharing in the self-exposure and, if you will, the sheer *risk* of Christ's *kenosis*. He enters into 'the radical and essential *solitude of man*—a solitude which was assumed by Christ and which, in Christ becomes mysteriously identified with the solitude of God.'[49] He becomes 'a poor man with the poor Christ.' In a sense, he has nothing to give: and we have seen that, according to Evdokimov, this means that all the monk has to share is his *being,* himself.

Here I should like to mention a passage in *The Sign of Jonas*,[50] the passage written a few days before his ordination to the priesthood, in which Merton reflects on the implications of his vocation to be a priest *and* a contemplative. The priestly state is itself a part of the contemplative life, 'an encounter of the substance of my soul with the living God';[51] and thus priesthood is intimately connected with that poverty which is a necessary condition of the contemplative state. 'To be a priest means, at least in my particular case, to have nothing, desire nothing, and be nothing but to belong to Christ.'[52] Priests who are contemplative monks must recognise 'that perhaps we have practically nothing to give to souls in the way of preaching and guidance and talent and inspiration. We are ashamed of any active apostolate that might conceivably come from us. And so we vanish into the Mass.'[53] The priestly contemplative is 'defined' by the Mass, by the representation of Christ's *kenosis* and sacrifice, and by nothing else, by no 'works,' no external apostolate; the priest lives Christ's sacrifice, or, rather, the kenotic Christ lives in the priest. We may compare another passage a little later on in *The Sign of Jonas,* written after Merton's ordination to the priesthood: 'Day after day I am more and more aware that I am anything but my everyday self at the altar.... I am superseded by One in whom I am fully real.... It is at Mass, by the way, that I am deepest in solitude and at the same time mean most to the rest of the universe. This is really the *only* moment at which I can give anything to the rest of men.'[54] And what is given is Christ, and therefore the self-in-Christ and the world-in-Christ.

Now I do not think that Merton is suggesting that the canonical state of priesthood is *necessary* for the full living of the contemplative life, but rather that 'being a contemplative' is a state of life which has 'priestly' implications. The priesthood of the contemplative or the solitary is a very different matter from the priesthood of the pastor, the teacher, the confessor, even if the contemplative is actually in priest's orders (Merton stresses, in the first of the passages to which I have referred,[55] that his interpretation of priesthood is a personal one, bound up with his *particular* vocation: 'Not all priests are necessarily committed, by their priesthood, to absolute poverty.'[56]) For the monk who is canonically a priest, his priestly *kenosis,* his gift of himself-in-Christ, is expressed pre-eminently in his offering of the Eucharist, but the significant element here is a *kenosis*, a poverty, which does not depend upon the rite of ordination. Evdokimov notes that 'The New Testament uses the term *presbuteros* to designate the particular ministry (the clergy) and keeps the term *hiereus* for the priesthood of the laity.... Christ abolished the *hiereus* as a distinct caste.'[57] There are, in fact, Evdokimov suggests, *two* priesthoods in the Church, the universal priesthood of the baptised, whose vocation is the consecration of all human existence, the offering of the whole of human being to God, and the 'functional' or 'ministerial' priesthood, whose vocation is to teaching, leading, and explicating the consecration of the world by the performance of the sacraments. The Christian layperson is *homo liturgicus,* the man whose whole life is directed to God, and who thus is able to direct all that is in his world to God, 'to be in love with all of God's creation in order to decipher the meaning of God in everything,'[58] 'Nature's Priest,' the 'interpretor' of creation to God. The priestly self-oblation of the believer becomes the vehicle of theophany in the world, we become transparent to God, and the light of the divine energy shining through us transfigures all things. Thus the *kenosis* of the contemplative is directly linked to the dignity of

33

the priest; the believer is baptized into the priesthood of Christ[59] as he or she is baptized into the *kenosis* of Christ; and so, finally, the universal priesthood of the laity is identical with the 'interiorized monasticism' of the laity.[60] The priest, the monk, the layperson (*'et hi tres unum sunt'*) holds the glass through which God sees the world and the world sees God.

'*Ses saints ne participent pas au dynamisme extérieur des événements ou, s'ils y participent, c'est autrement. Dostoievsky trace un visage de saint et le suspend au mur du fond comme une icone. Mais c'est à sa lumière révélatrice et thérapeutique qu'on déchiffre le sens des événements qui passent sur la scène du monde.*'[61] ['His saints do not participate in the outward dynamism of events; or if they do participate in them, it is in another fashion. Dostoevsky draws the face of a saint and hangs it on the back wall like an icon. But it is by means of its revelatory and therapeutic light that one deciphers the meaning of the events taking place on the world's stage.'] Thus Evdokimov, writing of the 'saints' in Dostoevsky's novels: the saint is an 'icon' not merely in the sense that he 'stands for' or 'witnesses to' the divine order, but because he is truly the channel through which God's energies enter into the human world. The saint's vision of the world is *God's* vision of the world, because the saint is 'transparent' to God: in the person of the saint contemplating God, God contemplates the world. This divine contemplation of the world is obviously not *reducible* to any fact in the world, it is a point of reference, in some sense 'outside' the world: hence the 'uselessness' of the saint, his position on the margin of human existence, his failure to provide practical solutions. Zossima in *The Brothers Karamozov* does not prevent the catastrophe that overtakes the Karamazov family; but it is his 'vision' of the situation that is ultimately the only real, credible, and stable factor in the working out of the brothers' destinies. Tikhon in *The Devils* fails to 'save' Stavrogin, who rejects his counsel in mingled fear and contempt; but again, Tikhon is the only character in the novel who is permitted to see Stavrogin whole, to see him as a person and a child of God. The Dostoyevskian saint is a sign of contradiction, a participant in the irony of the Incarnation: at once a fact in the world and a point outside it, useless, yet omnipercipient, the judge of the world and its savior, because he alone knows the 'truth' of the world, and his vision can restore it to a reality which is in accord with the purpose of God. His vision is, to take up a favorite expression of Evdokimov,

34

a vision of the 'sophianic' world, the world as first formed by the creative Wisdom of God, the world before the Fall. Of course, this conception is not an insight peculiar to modern Russian thought: in one form or another it is discernible throughout the Eastern patristic tradition, receiving what is probably its fullest and best formulation in the seventh century, in the writings of Maximus the Confessor. The task of Christian man is *reintegration,* the overcoming of the 'divisions' (*diaipeoeis*) caused by the Fall; these divisions are transcended in the first place by the Incarnation, and it is for each man in Christ to realize this victory in his own existence and so partake in the total restoration of the cosmos.[62]

If the restoration of the 'sophianic' world is such a fundamental constituent of the calling of every Christian, we might well expect to find Merton underlining its significance as part of his conception of monasticism as 'therapy' and 'humanization'; and, indeed, there is in his work an increasing interest in the priesthood of humanity in creation, and its corollary, the 'priesthood' of the monk and his reintegration of the world in God. In Merton's *Bread in the Wilderness* (1953), for example, there occurs this passage, so very reminiscent of Evdokimov: 'David is … filled with the primitive sense that man is the *Leitourgos* or the high Priest of all creation, born with the function of uttering in "Liturgy" the whole testimony of praise which mute creation cannot of itself offer to its God.'[63] The 'sophianic' theme is even more prominent in his discussion of *Doctor Zhivago*:[64] 'it is as artist, symbolist, and prophet that "Zhivago" stands most radically in opposition to Soviet society. He himself is a man of Eden, of Paradise. He is Adam, and therefore also, in some sense, Christ. Lara is Eve, and Sophia (the Cosmic Bride of God) is Russia.'[65] And 'One can see in Pasternak a strong influence from Soloviev's *Meaning of Love* and his theory of man's vocation to regenerate the world by the spiritualisation of human love raised to the sophianic level of perfect conscious participation in the mystery of the divine wisdom of which the earthly sacrament is love.'[66] And it is clear that this conception is one which Merton made very much his own in interpreting the monastic vocation: he can describe monasticism as 'recovery of paradisal simplicity,'[67] as 'incarnation and eschatology.'[68] 'Is it,' he asks, 'too romantic still to suppose the monk can bake the bread he will eat at table and consecrate on the altar—and *bake it well?*'[69] The monk's work, his shaping of the materials of the world, is not merely a prophylactic against *acedia,*

35

it is an integral part of his being-in-Christ, his sharing in the Word of Christ. To bake bread and bake it well, to till the soil, to carve wood or cast pots—all these are expressions of the monk's efforts to restore our use of created matter to its proper wholeness: Merton is even prepared to grant that 'The instinct that pushes modern monastic experiments toward salaried employment in industry is sure and authentic, though it raises special problems of its own.'[70] And here I must refer in passing to Merton's well-known interest in and admiration for the craftsmanship of the Shakers in their houses and domestic furniture—'a model of what the native American spirit can achieve in the monastic sphere.'[71] 'The Shaker builders—like all their craftsmen—had the gift of achieving perfect forms.'[72]

The monk, the *homo liturgicus,* is icon and iconographer: his material is himself and his personal world; and his 'holiness' and that of his world, the measure of their participation in the energies of God, are inseparable. The decay of Christian liturgical art always goes hand in hand with the degeneration of the spiritual life, just as the general decay of beauty and skill in human manufactures is bound up with a process of depersonalization in society at large, and if the Church cannot witness to the possibility of an integrated personal vision of reality in its art, who is there left who can?[73]

Evdokimov repeatedly associates the sterile individualistic emotionalism of late mediaeval and Counter-Reformation piety with the religiously barren and assertively secularist character of Renaissance and Baroque art,[74] and Merton says categorically that 'To *like* bad sacred art, and to feel that one is *helped* by it in prayer, can be a symptom of real spiritual disorders.'[75] This is not merely an incidental point: the refusal to bring one's full creative capacities to the service of God is a betrayal of the whole Christian calling to 'reintegration' of the world; it is 'a rank infidelity to God the Creator and to the Sanctifying Spirit of Truth,'[76] a reversion to slavery and inauthenticity. The Christian— and so, *a fortiori,* the monk—is bound to be an 'artist' in some way, a participant in the divine *poiesis*; and it is of great interest to compare what Merton has to say about the artist's (especially the poet's) vocation with his statement of the monastic vocation. The 'Message to Poets,'[77] read at a meeting of young Latin American (and some North American) poets in Mexico City in 1964, speaks of the poet's task in terms of the rejection of 'the political art of pitting one man against another and the commercial art of estimating all men at a price,'[78] the rejection of 'infidelity,' alienation, the experience of one's existence as 'betrayal.' The poet must not even let himself be defined by opposition to the false society, as this gives a definitive reality to the falsehood: 'Let us remain outside 'their' categories. It is in this sense that *we are all monks:* for we remain innocent and invisible to publicists and bureaucrats.'[79] If art is merely reaction against philistinism, it is wasted. In 'Answers on Art and Freedom'[80] (first published in a Latin American periodical), Merton contrasts the illusory freedom of the artist 'in revolt' against society, *defined* by his revolt and limited by it, who 'cultivates antiart as a protest against the art cult of the society in which he lives,'[81] with the true freedom which the artist should enjoy, 'freedom from the *internalized* emotional pressures by which society holds him down.'[82] As for the 'use' of art: 'The artist must serenely defend his right to be completely useless.'[83] 'Today the artist has, whether he likes it or not, inherited the combined functions of hermit, pilgrim, prophet, priest, showman, sorcerer, soothsayer, alchemist, and bonze. How could such a man be free? How can he really "find himself" if he plays a role that society has predetermined for him? The freedom of the artist is to be sought precisely in the choice of his work and not in the choice of the role of "artist" which society asks him to play.'[84] In other words, the dilemma of the artist is identical with the dilemma of the monk: each, at one level, rejects society, but has to guard against being defined by this rejection, against continuing to play a fore-ordained part (even though it be a 'negative' part) in the social myth. Or again, reverting to a theme discussed earlier in this essay, the monk or artist must beware of locating all the demons of the age outside himself: the artist, like the monk, has an interior wilderness to discover.

The importance of refusing the *role* of 'monk' or 'artist' lies in the corollary of this refusal, the affirmation of oneself simply as a person, as a human being: ultimately, I believe, it is this which is at the heart of the monastic theology of both Merton and Evdokimov. The monk is, quite simply, man-in-Christ engaging in his work as 'artist,' showing the world in its sophianic truth, by first confronting and rejecting the falsehood in society and in himself. We have seen Merton in particular speaking of the artist and the monk in closely similar terms: but finally the distinction must be drawn between the artist (simply *qua* artist) who, in some measure, is bound to be working 'in the dark,' and the monk who lives by the light of Christ.

Which is not to say that the monk's task is thereby made easier or its ends more obvious; only to recall that the monk knows himself to be sharing in a work of restoration whose extent neither his nor any other finite mind can grasp, the *anakephalaiosis* of all things in Christ. 'The necessary dialectic between eschatology and incarnation'[85] is a fundamental presupposition of all art; for the monk, it is given final and definitive shape in his baptism into the divine-human existence of the Incarnate Word, the Alpha and the Omega.

I have written throughout this paper of the monk as 'solitary.' I should perhaps say that I do not mean thereby to deny true 'monastic' significance to the cenobitic life. Far from it; I have, rather, followed Merton in presupposing that the *monachos*, if he takes his calling seriously, will inevitably be, in some degree, a 'solitary,' even if he is a member of a community, simply because the refusal of falsehood and the search for identity-in-God involve, by their very nature, a measure of solitude, a solitude often experienced as abandonment, dereliction. And it is equally important to bear in mind Merton's emphasis on the distinction between 'person' and 'individual' (a distinction very characteristic, as we have seen,[86] of Eastern thought) and the impossibility of attaining true personhood without existing in communion with others.[87] Again, bearing in mind Evdokimov's remarks about the 'provisional' character of monasticism, its dependence for its existence upon the imperfection of the present age,[88] I must make it clear that I have not intended to suggest that either Merton or Evdokimov believed the monastic *institution* to have been superseded, simply because the monastic state is seen by them as essentially identical with the calling of all Christians. In this age, the need for radical, concrete witness to the 'monastic' ideal by what I have called 'physical or geographical separation from society' is as great as ever. However, such a view of monasticism does raise very searching questions for the monastic institution and its attempts at renewal, questions which space (and incompetence) prevents me from entering into here. Perhaps, in conclusion, I may mention a third great theologian of the monastic life, whose name has constantly been in my mind as I write, because his writings seem in so many ways, to adumbrate the positions I have outlined here; I refer, of course, to Charles de Foucauld. To investigate the correspondence of his thought with that of Merton or Evdokimov, and to assess the extent of any influence he may have had upon them would be an undertaking far beyond my capabilities.

I mention this in the hope of illumination from those better quali-
fied, and in the conviction that it is to these 'Desert Fathers' of our
days that we must look for the most authentic statement of the es-
sentials of monasticism, and so also, the most fruitful source for a
theology of monastic renewal.

Chapter 3
'New Words for God':
Contemplation and Religious Writing

Early winter 1967, meal-cheese, bread, wine talk 3 hours.

Ralph Eugene Meatyard

'*We* are to be "new words for God" in that sense. And we celebrate Merton partly because of belief, which I think most Christians share, that the lives of certain people will become, in a very particular sense, "words of God." This life, this identity, this face, this voice, this "tonality" of being, becomes a word for God to us, a word God addresses to us.' (*See* p. 50)

Chapter 3
'New Words for God':
Contemplation and Religious Writing

The vision of the monk as fulfilling the 'poetic' vocation of human beings in a distinctive mode suggests some further examination of what Merton has to say about poetry. But if you look in Merton's work for definitions of poetry or of the poetic, you may sometimes be a little disappointed: as theologians have often found, it is quite difficult to give positive definitions of what matters most. You may find yourself defining more clearly by negations, by saying what you're not talking about. And what I want to begin with is four areas which Merton identifies as the sort of thing that poetry *isn't*.

As a way of finding a path into what he thinks about contemplation, I think this has its value. I'm relying here mostly on two quite familiar pieces, both reprinted in *Raids on the Unspeakable*: 'The Message to Poets' of 1964,[1] the short essay that was read at a meeting of Latin American poets in Mexico City in February of that year; and the 'Answers on Art and Freedom'[2] from around the same time, also written for a Latin American audience. Both texts clearly lay out not only what poetry isn't, but what it is that poetry is against.

First of all, poetry isn't, and is *against*, magic. Poetry is not about words that work. 'It is the businessman, the propagandist, the politician, not the poet, who devoutly believes in the magic of words,' writes Merton, 'For the poet, there is precisely no magic, there is only life in all its unpredictability and all its freedom. All magic is a ruthless venture in manipulation, a vicious circle, a self-fulfilling prophecy.' Words that 'work,' independent of their transparency to truth, are magical words. They live without anchorage in reality. They exist in order to exercise power, to control or develop a situation according to the will of the speaker.

Of course, there is an immediate relevance here to some of the unforgettable essays that Merton wrote in the middle sixties about the language of war, which for him was a cardinal example of magical language. You speak about war in such a way that the reality of conflict or of suffering is occluded. You speak about war in a way whose sole purpose is to create a consciousness like yours, another will projecting itself into the void. But I think too that Merton is casting a sidelong glance at some sorts of poetic self-consciousness, in the malign sense of the phrase—a poetic style that becomes self-referential, inclusive only of self. *That* sort of poetic freewheeling can be licensed as a parody of the unspeakable language of the state, 'The Ogre,' as W. H. Auden would have called it; but it isn't of itself the essence of poetry. And you might compare some remarks in 'Answers on Art and Freedom' on formalism, '... a meaningless cliché devised by literary and artistic gendarmes ... a term totally devoid of value or significance as are all the other cultural slogans invented in the police station.'[3]

Poetry then may at times be parodic and playful in order to show up what magical language is like, to expose the evils of the magical language of the state, or the military machine, or the police station. And somewhere in the background here is an allusion ringing off to Auden's short poem, already mentioned, written in 1968 after the invasion of Czechoslovakia, about 'the Ogre' striding across a plain covered with ruin and darkness. The Ogre has mastered everything except speech.

> The Ogre stalks with hands on hips
> While drivel gushes from his lips.[4]

Merton's 'Unspeakable' and Auden's 'Ogre' have a good deal in common.

Poetry isn't, and is against, magic and therefore, more generally, poetry isn't, and poetry is against, being useful, particularly that usefulness which we think of in terms of moralism. Here again, I turn to the Message to Poets:

> Let us not be like those who wish to make the tree bear its fruit first and the flower afterwards. A conjuring trick and an advertisement. We are content if the flower comes first and the fruit afterwards in due time.[5]

Useful moral poetry is an adjunct to something else. As poetry, it might be there or it might not. Poetry isn't and can't be decorative in that way and in that sense it's never simply rhetoric. It is never simply about persuading someone to do something or to think something: however significant the purpose, however good the end, poetry that is about defined goals, poetry that is functional, an advertisement, is betraying itself. And that phrase, 'a conjuring trick and an advertisement,' is very telling. Poetry which is an advertisement is poetry whose point is not *in itself.* This means that authentic poetry is *labour*, it's work: the doing of something which has its own integrity.

This leads me on to the third thing which poetry isn't and poetry is against. Poetry is against any focus on the artist rather than the work. To focus on the artist rather than the work is to draw our attention precisely to the manipulating, controlling will which is the enemy of all really truthful utterance. And I find myself turning, not wholly accidentally, once again to W. H. Auden. Auden was already a most austere critic of his contemporaries' poetry when he was an undergraduate, and there is a fine anecdote of an early encounter with Stephen Spender, who burst into Auden's room one day to say that he intended to be a poet when he grew up. Auden said, 'You mean you don't want to *write poetry*?'

This same emphasis comes out in a quite early letter to Mark Van Doren written in March 1948:

> I can no longer see the ultimate meaning of a man's life in terms of either 'being a poet' or 'being contemplative' or even in a certain sense 'being a saint,' (although that is the only thing to be). It must be something much more immediate than that. I—and every other person in the world—must say 'I have my own special peculiar destiny which no one else has had or ever will have. There exists for me a particular goal, a fulfilment which must be all my own—nobody else's—and it does not really identify that destiny to put it under some category—'poet,' 'monk,' 'hermit.' Because my own individual destiny is a meeting, an encounter with God that He has destined for me alone. His glory in me will be to receive from me something which He can never receive from anyone else.[6]

There is in this, of course, some of the ambiguous individualism that shadows a good deal of early and middle Merton, but the point stands. 'Being a poet,' 'contemplative,' or whatever is not what it's about, because this can direct attention once again to the will and psyche of the artist constructing a self. And there is a fundamental sense in which the will is inimical to art.

Finally, then, the fourth thing that poetry isn't, and poetry is against, is any sense of the self and its awareness that indulges the notion that we have indefinite choices. Poetry is against the romanticism of a will whirling in the void.

> The artist must not delude himself [writes Merton in *Answers on Art and Freedom*] that he has an infinite capacity to choose for himself and a moral responsibility to exercise this unlimited choice, especially when it becomes absurd.
>
> If he does this then let him take my word for it. He will find himself with the same problem and in the same quandary as those monks who have vegetated for three centuries in a mere morass of abstract voluntarism.[7]

The sense of indefinite choice, that the artist is someone with an infinite well of creativity which simply has to be activated in selecting what is to be uttered, focuses our attention once again on the role not the work, because work is always about *finite* choices. Labour is to do this rather than that, and to engage in the discipline and the limits of doing this rather than that. Work, labour, involves *local* commitment and specificity. Work is what has to be done in this moment, here and now, by this person, in the 'encounter' Merton speaks of in the letter to Mark Van Doren.

He speaks of 'this unique instant' in terms of 'the sense of water on the skin,'[8] a very powerful image. The poet acts, works, in that moment of contact with truth. And in another of the letters, this time to Sister Therese Lentfoehr, written in 1948, where he was obviously thinking quite a bit about this business of role and labour, he writes:

> With me, I know what the trouble is. I come upon a situation and the situation seems to require a poem. So I write a poem. But the poem turns out to be not the precise, individual poem which that specific situation had demanded from all eternity but just 'a poem.' A generic poem by Thomas Merton that is something like all the other poems by Thomas Merton and which he drags out of his stock to fit on every situation that comes along. That is why *Figures for an Apocalypse* is a whole string of complete misses. All I can say is that the arrows were in the general direction of some target or other but I'd be hard put to it to connect the firing with the real object that was there to be fired at.[9]

Time for one more reference to Auden, who speaks of the poem that presents itself and to which you have to say 'No longer, my dear,' and the one that comes along to which you have to say 'Not yet.'[10] 'Be a son of this instant,' writes Merton again in one of the texts reprinted in *Raids on the Unspeakable*, this time a text that emerges from his meditation on the Sufi mystic, Ibn Abbad.

So here are the four enemies of poetry; and a writing that avoids and resists those temptations and distortions will be, I want to suggest, *religious* writing. I hope you'll understand that as I develop these reflections, I'm using this phrase, 'religious writing,' to describe not writing about religious things but writing that is a religious *activity*; because what we have been looking at, the four things that poetry isn't, provides us with one way into understanding what writing might be when it is a religious labour. A writing that resists magic and will in their various disguises is writing that will allow truth, allow God. Or, to put it still more theologically, it is writing that aligns my action with *what is being done* in my environment. This is something totally different from passivity. Aligning one's action with what is being done in the environment is different from sitting there and saying 'let me be someone to whom things are done.' It is to require from me that most demanding of activities, the weaving in of my action with the action, the act, that is at work around in the universe: not passivity, but an attempt (to misuse the popular and rather horrible phrase), to be where action is. When we speak colloquially of 'being where the action is,' that's mostly the most appallingly trivial kind of aspiration we might have for our ego. Religious writing, poetry that is authentic religious writing, writing that is religious work, is very *precisely* an attempt to be where the action is, God's action, where *this* reality, me, my words, my perception, meet what is fundamental, God—the encounter spoken of in the letter to Mark Van Doren.

So that 'being a son of this instant'—in the phrase Merton adapts from Ibn Abbad—is encountering and entering into that elusive 'there before us' quality of God's action, that active reality—or, indeed, to use the scholastic language which was not at all alien to Merton's thinking, that 'pure act' which is beyond both memory and fantasy, the active 'being' of the world now, in this moment. Religious writing is an open door to what God is doing in making and loving the universe—which of course God does in every moment. Religious writing, writing that is religious work, is part of our attunement to the doing of God, made real and concrete here in how we see and how we attend: a loving and acting, a perceiving without egotistic will, but without passive resignation.

Now it is this attunement to the 'pure act' of God that seems to me to be fundamental, in the last analysis, to all that Merton says about the activity of poetic writing. But it is precisely here that you touch the unity of what Merton has to say about poetry and what Merton has to say about contemplation. I don't think I need to labour the point too much, but in order to come around at it by another route, I shall step back a little and look at one or two of the things which the tradition tells us about contemplation. Let us look at St John of the Cross for a moment, and particularly at a passage which grows and grows in my imagination as the years go by in *The Ascent of Mount Carmel,* where St John describes the process of contemplation, the process of growth into God's fullness, as a total restructuring of our inner life. Memory, understanding, and will are transformed into faith, hope, and love.[11] The renewed self or heart or imagination which has embarked upon the contemplative journey becomes *hopeful.* It becomes open to God's future. It becomes *faithful*; that is it becomes trustful in what it can't perceive or control. It becomes *lovingly attentive to truth.* All very splendid; and the bad news is of course, that this entails the blockage and frustration of the ways in which our human faculties habitually work, the Night of the Senses and of the Spirit; because in this process the ordinary objects of memory, understanding, and will disappear. That's to say, my awareness of myself, the way I build up a picture of myself from memory, self-perception, becomes blurred. I don't quite know who I am. My understanding meets a brick wall. I don't know what I am supposed to be engaging with. And my will is radically paralysed and frustrated, because there is no way in which I can impose what I want or prefer on the situation I am in. My only way through is for memory, understanding, and will to become hope, faith, and love. And this dismantling of the imagination and its reconstructing by the gift of God in darkness is by no means distant from what Merton has to say about overcoming the false poetic consciousness—about what poetry isn't, and what it's against.

Memory can be the conscious self-indulgence of a role, the

48

clear sense of who and what I am. I am 'a poet'—and, one of these days, I'll get around to writing some poetry. False poetic activity is about justifying what is being done, being useful, getting people to do things, to have the right ideas and do the right actions. Faith is about justification by God and by Grace. The will can turn in on its own fantasies of being a kind of creative abyss out of which come constant, endless, infinite new things; and this will must be translated into the labour of love, attention to the instant, to what God does now.

It seems to me then that Merton probably could not have written precisely what he did about true and false poetry without, at the back of his mind, some very deep awareness of what the contemplative transformation involved. All real poets know that. Merton had read his John of the Cross of course, and knew it better than most; so that, at the heart of what I want to say is that we will understand best the point of contact, the point of convergence between Merton on poetry and Merton on contemplation, when we put side by side Merton's negative theology of poetry as expressed in the 'Message to Poets' and the negative vision of John of the Cross; both of them being about attunement to the act of God there before you in every instant, the act of God which neither memory nor fantasy, neither images of the past nor images of the future can capture; the act of God which can only be apprehended by a particular kind of costly openness, which refuses the comforts of memory and the comforts of fantasy in order to 'be' where we are.

And from that new imagination come 'New Words for God.' That bit of my title is more ambiguous than might at first appear. Obviously new words for God emerge from this process because on the far side of what I have been talking about, God's act can be spoken of in and by my attunement to it, by words that make room for attention; which is why God is spoken of, and spoken for, or indeed just spoken, precisely in writing that has no explicitly religious content, because of the character of the writing as a labour of the instant. 'New words for God' then, on the far side of the negative theology, will be words that have room for the act of reality, the 'there-before-us' reality which is God's act in the present moment. And the religious writing that is, in the more obvious sense, words for God, will be precisely those words that escape the prisons, or the possible prisons, of memory and fantasy as we normally use those categories.

Equally though, 'New Words for God' could be understood in a rather different sense. The poet and/or contemplative becomes herself a new word for God. In the act of challenge and suspension of the will, of the controlling ego, the life, the concrete identity of the poet and the contemplative, becomes itself Word, becomes itself a communication. It is God acting. Merton's own interest in the Eastern Christian tradition justifies some connections being made between this vision of the poet and the contemplative and the deep-rooted Eastern Christian idea that the 'logos' of each item in the universe is the utterance of the Logos of God in a particular and unique way. And I think back again to the letter to Mark Van Doren: '[God's] glory in me will be to receive from me something he can never receive from anyone else because it is a gift of his to me which he has never given to anyone else and never will.'[12]

We are to be 'new words for God' in that sense. And we celebrate Merton partly because of the belief, which I think most Christians share, that the lives of certain people will become, in a very particular sense, 'words for God.' This life, this identity, this face, this voice, this 'tonality' of being, becomes a word from God to us, a word God addresses to us.

Poetry and contemplation, both identifying, sketching or pointing to what it might be for God to find words in the world, alike challenge other kinds of words for God, old words for God, safe words for God, lazy words for God, useful words for God. I taught Christian doctrine for many years and I'm not going to cut away the ladder on which I climbed; but it seems to me that Christian doctrine is essentially there in order that we may grasp how God acts in creating and transfiguring. Christian doctrine exists so that certain obstacles may be taken away to our openness to the action of God. We *need* Christian doctrine because we need some notion of what it is we are trying to be attuned to. Attunement to a void isn't very much use, and out of that come other kinds of unspeakable language. But if doctrine doesn't make possible poetry and contemplation, then doctrine is a waste of time; it becomes purely and simply old, safe, and useful. Which is where the poetic and contemplative touch the *prophetic*, because the prophetic is all about the diagnosis of dead words and false acts. The prophetic task is to smell out death in a situation.

In conclusion: I've tried to sketch a negative theology of the poetic, and I've preferred that, as a way in, to a positive definition of the poetic—not simply because I find Merton's positive definitions of the poetic occasionally a bit disappointing, but because most people who try to find words for God are likely to be more acutely aware of what it is they *mustn't* do than what it is they must do or say. This doesn't mean that we privilege inarticulacy or even silence. It does mean, though, that poetic and contemplative language, the struggle to find new words for God and to understand that the nature of religious writing, of writing as religious activity, is nothing if not a deeply self-critical enterprise, a living under judgement. But this is only another way of saying that these are activities which we can't begin to grasp or get any purchase on, without the vivid and sometimes frightening sense of what they are open to. The poet and the contemplative alike live under a very broad sky—which is sometimes a night sky. The attempt to build shelters or dig holes, the attempt to draw helpful charts of the sky which will allow you to find your way around, is a seduction that is always present. Perhaps the most important thing we can do if we are at all interested in the language of poetry and contemplation is to set up warning signs on our desks and our altars and our *prie-dieux*; yet to know at the same time that these are not warning signs telling us about the punishments for making a mistake, but *reminders* of how very easily we become prisoners of the controlling will that we love and indulge—and how very bad such a prison is for any of us.

Chapter 4
'The Only Real City':
Monasticism and the Social Vision

«Wisdom will honor you if you embrace her/she will place on your head a fair garland/she will bestow on you a crown of glory.» (Proverbs 4: 8-9)

ΑΓΙΑΣΟΦΙΑ

HAGIA SOPHIA

¶ . . . One day/Father Louis (Thomas Merton) our friend/came from his monast at Trappist/Kentucky/to bring an ill novice to the hospital in Lexington. (J had known Father Louis since 1955 when J visited him for the first time. Later we pr ed several of his books.) We had prepared a simple luncheon and J welcomed h to sit with us at table. From where he sat he had a good view of the triptych on the chest and he often looked at it. After a while he asked quite abruptly/«And is the woman behind Christ?» J said/«J do not know yet.» Without further que tion he gave his own answer. «She is Hagia Sophia/Holy Wisdom/who crowns Christ.» And this she was — and is.

54

Chapter 4
'The Only Real City':
Monasticism and the Social Vision

Transformed language, language delivered from prison, necessarily means transformed relations. What we have just been exploring in connection with honest and dishonest language relates directly to Merton's developing reflections on honest and dishonest community. 'This is the only real city in America'; Merton's first reaction to the Abbey of Gethsemani, recorded in his *Secular Journal* for 7 April 1941[1] casts a teasing light on some of his reflections on monastery and society in the early sixties. It is a significant phrase to use, though. In this last period before entering Gethsemani, Merton seems to have been turning his mind to questions about true and false community to the contrast between the pseudo-cities of modern America and their dreadful parodic image in the streets of Harlem, where those who are not really citizens are herded together within sight of prosperity and stability and left to die. As the journal finishes, he is trying to get clear whether his choice is indeed between Harlem and Gethsemani. And the consciously dramatic framing of this question at the end of the Journal suggests that in the middle fifties, when this material was polished for publication, he was still thinking about his vocation in terms of where the 'real' city was to be found.

What changed in the early sixties? This is very clearly the period in which the role of the 'guilty bystander' was shaped, the period which saw the writing of most of what became *Conjectures*. I want to point to a few factors in the early sixties that may help explain something of the drastic shift going on—factors which arise primarily from Merton's reading, but which are immediately intensified by biographical and historical currents, his worsening relationship with the monastic hierarchy and the mounting crisis over racial exclusion in the USA with its attendant violence. The private journals are of cardinal importance here; but there are things in *Conjectures* that are, oddly not to be found in the journals, above all the very substantial discussions of Bonhoeffer, which contribute much insight.

The first factor is one that we encounter early in the journals for 1960. In May and June, he was reading Hannah Arendt's *The Human Condition*, and, as Michael Mott recognises in his biography,[2] Merton found this work profoundly unsettling. It is one of the books in which Arendt sets out her conviction that Christianity had a near-fatal effect upon the whole idea of civic life: classical civilisation had understood the polis as the 'space' in which human beings exercise their freedom for meaningful co-operative action, for work towards those goods that need plural agents working in harmony to secure them; but the Christian suspicion of 'the world' leads to an undervaluing of strictly political action of this sort. The active life becomes a generalised set of responses to the affairs of the world, and the distinctive vocation of the classical city disappears.[3]

In the fourth volume of the journals (published as *Turning Towards the World*) Merton picks up the idea of space in which intelligible interactions with other free adults may happen, and ruefully asks (in the light of a frustrating attempt to telephone his publisher) whether his own spiritual space is really New York, the world of professional and straightforward business dealing;[4] but he returns in mid-June,[5] to develop a fuller response which almost turns Arendt on her head. The book challenges the historic conviction of the supremacy of contemplation over action—but it does so on the basis of regarding contemplation as a distant relation from which certain kinds of provocative wonder are absent. Merton, however, sees it as 'the deepest and most important defence of the contemplative life that has been written in modern times.'[6] What he means by this is clear from his summary of Arendt's arguments: the active life degenerates when it is separated from its roots in proper (wondering) contemplation, and turns into activity whose goal is simply to forward a process. And to elevate the contemplative in such an environment is to miss the point: in a world in which there is not enough free and adult engagement with reality in the company of other free agents, it is positively damaging to behave as if the real problem were 'worldliness.' We are not worldly enough. As Arendt concludes, we have made ourselves a culture in which the genuinely public has virtually disappeared in favour of the 'social'—the universal housekeeping that has replaced the classically demarcated spheres of public and domestic. In the classical world, politics was grounded in the public debate about values and the nurturing of admirable public lives, generous and deserving of imitation; the domestic real was the 'hidden' sphere of managing the necessities. Modernity (distorted by the Christian heritage) has no real debate about values, no concept of public greatness, and a focus on management and process.

Hence Merton in turn concludes that the task of the modern contemplative is to expiate this history and recover the sense of public greatness—not public success but something of the Aristotelian (and Thomist) vision of greatness of soul. It is not that the contemplative repudiates the 'process' but that s/he learns how to control it, thus reasserting the value of the unique individual as the necessary element in the construction of public order and public health.[7] Merton takes the whole discussion off in a direction by no means obviously signalled in Arendt's schema, identifying the process as that which inevitably destroys the properly personal and sees—for example—holiness as lying in the satisfaction of certain conditions that can be specified as abstract. And so we begin to see emerging in Merton's response to what was evidently a crucial book for him an implicit notion of the contemplative community as a true polis—but in quite a different sense from the one suggested in the *Secular Journal*. The civic excellence he discerned in Gethsemani in 1941 had a great deal to do with the vision of the monastery as a perfect productive unit, making excellent things ('bread, cheese, butter ...';[8] he would live to regret this positive evaluation of the cheese) because its work was a sort of solemn play, a form of labour that was not dictated by considerations of effectiveness and purposefulness and so was supremely effective and purposive. Merton in these pages is suitably careful about not identifying the excellence of the abbey with its external beauty and order. What matters is the motivation, the doing of ordinary things well because they are done for a purpose beyond the practical, done as 'a mixture of penance and recreation.'[9] But what is missing in this account, intriguing in itself, is the ideal Arendt sketches of a space for free collaboration, discourse, shared self-definition.

And such a reimagining of the civic aspect of contemplative life leads Merton to an impatience more marked than ever with myths of the Christian *civitas*. By July 1961, he has moved on significantly from some of what his first reading of Arendt had suggested. He had toyed[10] with the idea that figures like de Gaulle and St Louis of France could be held up as models of Christian 'great souls'; but in his entry for 7 July 1961 he questions whether even these really represent a Christian civic virtue that can be treated as an indestructible paradigm.[11] By 23 February, 1963, this has become a sharply hostile critique of the ideal of 'Christian civilisation,' as exemplified precisely by de Gaulle and by the appeal to a lost Christian Europe, to the ghost of Charlemagne. Christian witness in the *polis* is more necessary than ever; but 'Christian policy' is a dangerous chimera, given the actual record of professing Christians in the management of public affairs.

Here then is one determining element in Merton's progress in the sixties towards open intervention in the public sphere. But it is evidently sharpened, even embittered, by his growing sense of the monastery not as an exemplary *civitas* but as a polity all too clearly operating like other political societies. In the late summer of 1960, he is struggling, not very articulately, with the contradictions of a life in which he has been forced to recognise the falsity of rejecting 'worldly' political commitment, yet lives in an institution where he both has to accept the clichés of conventional American politics (the monks' vote for the right professional candidate—Kennedy—is assiduously sought) and to hold back from anything that could be called political action. 'I am in effect a political prisoner at Gethsemani,' he writes with characteristic drama;[12] then, equally characteristically, identifies his own complicity in this, the degree to which it suits him.

Protests about the 'secular' atmosphere of the monastery and the Order multiply as the journal proceeds,[13] and August 1961 sees a particularly savage note prompted by the reading of a refectory book on convent life ('an immoral book,' one that glorifies conformity and repression under a 'coy' and winsome style).[14] Not coincidentally, the entry for two days later reflects on the secularisation of monastic time:[15] the sacred world of traditional practice, contemplation, meaningful labour and liturgy, is undermined by secular attitudes to technologised production and pointless reform of the timetable. Organise the practical side of monastic life, and there is proper space for the sacred—regarded as another, parallel, world of performance and production (an occasion for another very Mertonian broadside about the choir).[16] Later on (October 1962), Merton has a telling comparison between how the world views the USA and how a community views an abbot whose exercise of power has become stale and resented; obedience is exacted on the basis of the promises and slogans of years ago, but while it still commands conformity (the power is indisputable), it cannot command love. It is a prescient picture of American hegemony, and we shall be returning to the theme; but it is also a revealing glimpse of the politics of the monastery in general and Gethsemani in particular.

In short, Merton has come to believe that the monastic life as he is living it fails in the distinctive vocation that is given to monasticism in the modern age, the vocation he decodes from Hannah Arendt. It is secular in the wrong ways and unworldly in the wrong ways. Because it reproduces the anxiety, the disillusion, the empty speech of the culture around, it offers no hope of transformation; because it repudiates 'the world' in order to maintain a space of its own, it cannot give space to a world which is in urgent need of authentically political discourse and exchange. Merton was obviously moved and engaged by aspects of Bonhoeffer's dissolution of the conventional Church-world divide, quoting[17] Bonhoeffer's remarkable claim in his prison letters that 'the Church alone offers any prospect for the recovery of the sphere of freedom (art, education, friendship, and play, "aesthetic existence" as Kierkegaard called it). . . . What man is there among us who can give himself with an easy conscience to the cultivation of music, friendship, games or happiness? Surely not the ethical man, but only the Christian.' Freed from the crushing and resentful sense of self-conscious obligation that weighs on the 'ethical' person, the believer has space for the cultivation of the human (though compare this with a passage[18] on how ethical concepts made 'homeless' by modern barbarism return for shelter to the Church). It is a curious echo of that fleeting insight in the *Secular Journal* about monastic work as playful as well as penitential. The impatience about monastic subculture has to do with a recognition that, once monastic life and work become dutiful and profitable, an aspect of a successful corporate identity, it has ceased to be a truly alternative politics.

But how to become sufficiently worldly and sufficiently unworldly in the monastery. One of Merton's greatest gifts in the sixties—indeed throughout his life—was his ability to analyse cliché; and he is self-aware enough to know that mere counter-cultural noises will not necessarily escape the trap of cliché, mirroring the dead discourse of the established mainstream. 'The question is—how to clearly, definitely, and openly make such a stand without lending oneself to exploitation by one or other of the big power groups,' Merton asks in April 1961 in relation to clarifying a position about opposition to nuclear armaments.[19] Taking a stand by means of a published statement is, surely, all that is possible; but it is a necessary step in 'fulfilling my obligations as a human being in the present crisis' (August 1961)[20]—and this is an early reaction to the 1962 prohibition of publishing on the nuclear issue—may it not be that the obligation to 'form a judgement' or take a stand is a lesser obligation than the search for inner truthfulness?[21] 'We are tempted to do anything as long as it seems to be good' when we begin to recognise the corruption and emptiness that hides within our well-intentioned efforts. And he has already noted in early 1962[22] the seductive pressure to 'say something,' to collude with the messianic expectations of various different 'publics,' in and out of the peace movement. These observations follow closely on his notes about a letter from Czeslaw Milosz responding to his early articles on peace: reading between the lines, it seems as though Milosz has warned about the danger of facile sloganeering on peace as on other subjects, and about the risks of making polarisation worse. 'There are awful ambiguities in this peace talk,' Merton admits, and he wonders if he has been writing 'noble nonsense';[23] a few weeks later, he mentions 'weariness of words' in the same context.[24] Yet he is not willing simply to accept Milosz's criticisms as invalidating his own sense of an imperative somewhere in this. You cannot turn away from action, but not all action is wise or creative: what might right action be for a contemplative?[25] There is cause for caution about the mixture in the peace movement of 'moral sloppiness' and proper and generous protest.[26]

Perhaps, Merton ventures the goal is not statement but 'silent and conclusive action' and 'meaningful suffering,' that is, frustration accepted in freedom.[27] And when he tries to think this through more fully, at some point in August 1962,[28] he acknowledges the risks of treating the peace question as one of theory, an attractive idea which allows for the exercise of aggressive, adversarial, fundamentally insecure posturing. Non-violence must be studied carefully, but then realised in the details of monastic life: 'Short of this, the monastic life will remain a mockery in my life.' The point is in fact made earlier, rather poignantly, in the journals,[29] this time in the wake of thinking about Zen: 'Perhaps peace is not something you "work for." It either is or it isn't. You have it or not. If you are at peace there is peace in the world. Then share your peace with everyone and the world will be at peace.'

Whether Merton discovered how to achieve this 'silent and conclusive action' is hard to discern. The problems of 1965, when his relations with some in the peace movement were complex and strained near to breaking point, the 1967 exchange with Rosemary Ruether—these point very clearly to the continuing ambiguities in his witness. Despite what sounds like a commitment to 'civil disobedience' in 1962,[30] apparently involving a commitment to some sort of passive resistance to injustice within the monastic system, he was never easy about direct action. In a shrewd essay of 2000 on Merton's vision of the city,[31] Gary Hall, a Methodist minister working in situations of extreme urban deprivation, notes that Merton underrates the cathartic effects of direct action, even what seems to be violent action, in releasing tension. It may not be good in itself, but Merton's critique of it 'betrays his distance,'[32] and does less than justice to his basic insights about the city as space for meaningful action (Hall does not mention the Arendt discussions, but the connections are evident). But allowing for all these reservations and complexities the very fact of Merton's agonised and inconsistent self-questioning, the apparent resolutions and radical second thoughts, might be thought to add up to a particular kind of public intervention, not planned or structured in any of the ways Merton himself thought about, yet with its own authority. As so often in Merton, when you are inclined to think that he has settled for a dramatic and faintly delusory self-image, you discover, sometimes within a few pages (as will have become clear from a good many of the texts referred to here), that he has spotted the false note himself and moved on. The silent action is not so much a coherent form of witness, satisfactory to Merton and his imagined public, as a consistent habit of turning on his own language, his own 'scripts,' in the name of a better truthfulness.

But the feeling after a 'silent action,' the longing for a life that will exhibit another order for the city, needs to be read also against the background of a second set of factors in Merton's intellectual discoveries in the early sixties. The very first page of *Conjectures* uses a word that will not have been very familiar to his readers: writing (memorably) about Karl Barth and Mozart, he speaks of Barth's daily listening to Mozart as an attempt 'to awaken, perhaps, the hidden sophianic Mozart in himself, the central wisdom that comes in tune with the divine and cosmic music and is saved by love, yes, even by eros.' 'Sophianic': the word reflects the fact that, when the original journal note on this was written (September 1960[33]), Merton had been reading a book by the French Orthodox theologian Olivier Clément, *Transfigurer le temps*,[34] which had undoubtedly revived his earlier fascination with the notion, particularly strong in some modern Russian writers, of Sophia, the personified divine wisdom that pervades creation. He had read a little of the work of Sergii Bulgakov by 1959 (see, for example, the journal references in April 1957[35]) when he spelled out in a letter to Victor Hammer something of Bulgakov's enormous intellectual scheme centring upon Sophia[36] and by 1963 he had written his celebrated prose poem on the subject. But I suspect that the reading of Clément[37] had taken Merton's understanding of the theme in a new direction. He has picked up from Clément the point that our fallen experience of time is always bound up with absence; the restoration of the divine image is a discovery or recovery of the radiance of a present moment, the ordinary world of humanity here and now transfigured by transparency to God. 'The Christian struggles,' wrote Clément, 'to transform the earth into a sacrament, to transform culture into an icon of the heavenly Jerusalem.' The holiness that the believer seeks is never something sought for an individual: it is a matter for sadness so long as it is not shared by all, so that one of the characteristic features of true holiness is an expectant waiting for the sanctification of others.[38] This is what gives the saints the strength to resist all penultimate political solutions, all totalitarianisms. Time becomes, for the Christian, both a perpetual present and a time of positive expectation—a paradox, but a true one, recognising that the repose and stability of the saint is also, while the world lasts, a looking forward to the act that God alone can bring to completion beyond our history. So, a dynamic, but also a detachment that allows immersion in the actually present; a powerful model for Merton to absorb, and I believe that at this juncture the deeper discovery of this eastern idiom was a significant aspect of his new valuation of the space of the common life in the monastery and beyond, his search for an honest form of 'silent action'—though the ambiguity of talking of 'silence' here will need some further comment.

But it is another Orthodox writer who makes for Merton a further connection. In July 1963 (as noted in chapter 2), he is reading an article by Paul Evdokimov on early monasticism; and later Evdokimov's vision is placed, significantly, towards the end of *Conjectures of a Guilty Bystander*, as if to indicate that it can be read as something of a climactic point. He is struck by the Russian's description of monasticism as something that does not situate itself on the edge of the world, but 'in the face of the world.' In the journal, Merton thinks first—understandably, perhaps—of the temptations here, the seduction of making a pseudo-society to replace the one you have left. But by the time he has written this up in *Conjectures*, he has integrated the argument far more fully into his own perspective. 'The monastic consciousness of today in America is simply a marginal worldly consciousness';[39] the monasticism Evdokimov writes about is a phenomenon that proclaims the end of history, in the sense of making manifest the hidden dimensions of history. It does not situate itself in a tactfully remote and fairly safe corner of the secular map, but ignores the terms of secular territory and simply displays humanity as it 'pre-historically' is. Thus the monk who acts 'on' the world from a vantage point outside,[40] but someone who lives and acts out of the depths of the world, the centre of the world.

Merton remains in some respects cautious, but it is clear that he has been marked by Evdokimov's argument. Even if the 'desert phase' is over in monastic history (and Evdokimov, as we have seen, devoted great energy to arguing that the appropriate form of monastic commitment today was not celibate separation but an 'interiorised' monasticism that had been taught by the desert monks about the proper 'locus' of Christian discipleship, at the heart of the world, within and beyond history), the radical summons to another truth at the heart of what we think we see remains. Something has been uncovered in the laboratory of the desert which now has to be lived out in new forms. And, as Merton stresses in *Conjectures*, that discovery is primarily about the need for the monk to 'vomit up the interior phantom, the doubter, the double'—that is the shadowy self-image which can so easily be concealed under the ascetic cloak, which becomes a means of establishing one's own rightness.[41] Unless this image is purified, monasticism becomes another illusory 'city': 'One lives marginally, with one foot in the general sham. Too often the other foot is in a sham desert, and that is the worst of all.'[42]

So the insight that saw the monastery as a true city was not one that Merton ever abandoned; and the social critique of the mid-sixties especially grew out of the sense of obligation Merton evidently felt to speak for true civic identity, this being the job that the contemporary Christian has most indisputably been given. What we witness as he tries to find ways of speaking with integrity in such a context is a painful lack of clarity about what action (including speech) is really possible for the monk—particularly the monk as construed by modern Catholic convention. The monastic identity against which Merton is rebelling is one in which unworldliness is a mixture of proclaimed cultural detachment and unconscious reproduction of the prevailing cultural norms. There is thus no new world announced by the modern monastery. And the same is true, *mutatis mutandis*, of the modern Church, which faces exactly the same problem of false detachment and false conformity together. To define the place where the Church or the monastery or the individual ascetic may settle with a reasonable degree of security is to accept the terms on which the godless world works. The paradox is that when the Church and the monastery accept their 'homelessness' in the world, accept that Christendom will not return and there is only a minority future,[43] they are free to offer a far more comprehensive and hopeful vision. The vision is not of the possibility of a secure enclave, an Indian reservation in the modern world, but of a genuinely civic and political life open to all, and a vision of the material world itself as sacramental; it is a reclaiming of the present, the prosaic, the human.

And as such it is also a place where speech becomes possible again. The secure enclave will either speak a hermetically sealed dialect or it will speak a version of the tired and empty language of politics in the world around. The true city is a place where language is restored; where language is not about manipulating signs to secure submission or compliance but an exchange of the perceptions of free persons, seeking to discover what can be done in common, what the goods are that can be sought together. Merton in these years is beginning to refine his ear for self-serving nonsense, for poisoned language. He notes in September 1961[44] that he and the abbot lack a common language and meet only 'in the realm of perfectly acceptable clichés. Not cliché words but cliché ideas.' In the light of his deeper commitment to the monastery as a place of renewed public speech, this is more than just a complaint about relations with authority. And his crossness about the drive for liturgical reform[45] is less about the content of new liturgical composition than about the glib slogans used to promote it.

It is, of course, Hannah Arendt's account of the Eichmann trial that prompts some of his most searching thoughts on false and diseased speech. Eichmann's remarks as he faces execution are a perfect embodiment of dead language—or rather not so much dead as lethal, infecting the world with death, in their flat denial of moral depth, guilt, memory, history itself, we might say. In *Conjectures*,[46] Merton elaborates his briefer comments in *Turning Towards the World*[47] with the prophetic warning that we have not seen the last of Eichmann. Eichmann's astonishing platitude at the foot of the gallows ('After a short while, gentlemen, we shall all meet again. Such is the fate of all men.') is heard by Merton as a promise that our future will be full of Eichmanns; in these words, the technological mass murderer blithely identifies himself with his executioners and warns that his name is legion.

We looked earlier in this book at the echoes we find in Merton of Auden's powerful little poem about Czechoslovakia in 1968: Merton is contemplating a monster who 'cannot master speech': 'The Ogre stalks with hands on hips. / While drivel gushes from his lips.' The resonance is clear with Merton's prose-poetic work of the middle sixties as it appears in, for example, *Raids on the Unspeakable* (especially 'Atlas and the Fatman'). And if speech is a casualty of the politics of the self-enclosed world, it is obvious that for the Christian, and the monk in particular, a central aspect of the Christian renewal of the space of public exchange has to be a renewal of language. Merton has no option but to 'break silence,' from this perspective. As we have seen, the pitfalls of interventions in spoken and written form became very more familiar to Merton, and he is drawn by the model of 'silent action' and the pursuit of an inner resolution; but there is no obvious way around the challenge to act so as to make something different happen in words.

In poetry, yes; perhaps in some sorts of direct and personal exchange; in proper liturgy. But the difficulties Merton faces are very like those analysed so unforgettably by Bonhoeffer in his prison letters; the words of faith are too well-known to believers for their meaning to be knowable. And outside the language of faith, the temptations are to use your words as a demonstration of individual drama, an indulgence of the ego. Caught between clichés and posturings, what is the believer to do? Merton has set himself the problem that was to shape his work from the early sixties onwards. And, tellingly, it is far from clear whether we can say that he ever arrived at a resolution; what matters is that his practice as a writer, privately in the journals and publicly, shows why the question is serious. He acknowledges that almost any words in the modern cultural setting will be worn and shabby or illusory and self-serving. When the public space has been so eroded, it is not surprising if we cannot find words appropriate for free people; and the modern monastery, with its second-hand, unnoticed worldliness and its confusions about time and liturgy, has no authentic words to help. But what the monastic life can still do, it seems, is to sustain lives that will not be content with clichés, even if they do not know how to avoid them. As has already been hinted, the speech that is called for is not—though Merton's romanticism pushed him quite near to seeing this as the ideal—a purified transparent language, but rather a record of recognising the failures without yielding to them or treating them as natural.

When we read the later Merton, we need to be careful about rushing to identify this or that as an example of a 'prophetic' voice. Merton certainly spoke words of uncomfortable truth to the systems of his day, yet he also drew back from binding himself to words and actions that threatened to become the breeding ground for new clichés. He wrote finely on war and peace and the nuclear menace; but he declined finally to become a house guru for the peace movement, in ways that could annoy and disturb his friends as well as his critics. The remarkable and often-noted thing about so much of his massive correspondence is its 'ventriloquial' character: he speaks uncannily with the voice of whomever he is writing to, from Sufi scholar to teenage girl. And while this undoubtedly has something to do with his passion for approval and acceptance, it is also a mark of his reluctance to commit his deepest identity to one voice only. Of course, it is a deeply ambiguous feature of his own writing, but it is also connected with a self-critical grasp of his own speech: he does not and cannot simply develop a single Mertonian register (though every reader will know how utterly distinctive and recognisable he can be), but plays with the tone and vocabulary of his partners in speech, both to say what he knows he has to say and to discover something else, something not knowable or expressible in one consistent voice alone.

Perhaps a monastery—or a church—might be a place where there is time and room for people to explore each other's languages like that, delivered from the oppressive need to refine and concentrate one authoritative voice, whether the individual's or the institution's. And perhaps it is in this way that—picking up Bonhoeffer's insight—that cultural and moral seriousness, driven out from the vulgarised and over-managed modern social world, finds a proper home in the Christian community. But there is one last turn to the argument. Put in the way I have just expressed it, there is a manifest danger of a sort of dilettantism: the Church as a protracted seminar on human good. We have to remember that the exchange and exploration of Mertonian conversation is not exempt from the pervasive risk of self-serving that belongs to human beings in virtue of their fallen state, the shadow that language itself carries in a world of power, greed, and self-protecting images. Late in 1963,[48] Merton contemplates Barth's startling definition of being human as standing where Jesus is, 'as a bearer of the wrath of God.' Being human is to be, down to the very root, under wrath—that is incapable of assuring ourselves of God's favour, alienated from who we are in God's purpose. God alone can assure us; but to hear that assurance we must know what wrath means. 'I think I will have to become a Christian,' Merton muses, having read Barth on Jesus' encounter with Pilate, which according to Barth says everything that needs to be said about the Church and the *polis*.[49] Politics—in the ordinary sense—in the Church, the Church pretending to engage with the world by cautious public pronouncement, above all the reduction of the gospel to specific contemporary agendas, all this is what Barth memorably calls 'the dog in the nice room,' the presence guiltily slinking in where it doesn't belong. In contrast, the real preacher of the gospel knows that humanity, totally under wrath is also totally taken to the far side of that wrath because it is absorbed in Jesus and there is no going back: Jesus' victory is the only truly serious thing and everything else can be looked at with patience and humour.

No account of Merton's wrestling with the political vocation can ignore this. In these thoughts on one particular period in Merton's evolution, I have been trying to understand him as finding a way within a territory mapped out with reference by three points of orientation: to Arendt, to Clément and other Orthodox writers, and to Bonhoeffer and Barth. The Christian life has to justify its implicit claim to be the true 'civic' existence, a space for the conversation of free people; it is equipped for this by the grace of experiencing a true present, a sophianic depth in things; and, for it not to be a static ideological construction, confident that it has found a definable sacred space to occupy and defend, it must be permeated with the knowledge of 'wrath' always present, always overcome—an utterly inescapable human failure that is repeatedly made the material of God's work and so cannot be absolutised or accepted with resignation. The civic language of Christianity seeks to utter all this. Merton's many voices and many turnings and returnings on himself exhibit some of what this civic language might be.

A last image. So much of this discussion has been about territories and spaces in one way and another, and about the dangers of territories defended, walled off, in ways that stifle the vision of active common humanity. Early in *Turning Towards the World*, in an entry in July 1960,[50] Merton comments on the mounting crisis in Cuba, and the USA's determination to hold on to one of its military bases at all costs, against the will of Castro's government. In the context of Merton's wider discussion of what is authentically political and civic, this is a significant issue, putting in question, as he sees it, the USA's own foundational vision and myths of political liberty and civic discourse (the Boston Tea Party, the Declaration of Independence). For the reader today, meditating on the anti-political and anti-civic pressures of our day, what leaps from the page is the name of the base: Guantanamo.

Chapter 5
'Not Being Serious':
Thomas Merton and Karl Barth[1]

'Everyone who has to contend with unbelief should be advised that he ought not to take his own unbelief too seriously. Only faith is to be taken seriously, and if we have faith as a grain of mustard seed, that suffices for the devil to have lost his game.' [*Karl Barth*, 1963] (*See* p. 73)

Chapter 5
'Not Being Serious':
Thomas Merton and Karl Barth[1]

Alongside Merton's obituaries in 1968, in many publications, appeared obituaries of a very different figure indeed—possibly the greatest Protestant thinker of the twentieth century: Karl Barth. I was at that time a first-year student of theology in Cambridge and during my first term I picked up the newly published British edition of *Conjectures of a Guilty Bystander*. (I paid forty-two shillings for it, nearly half my weekly budget at that time, which may suggest that I took Merton seriously even then.) And what are the first words of *Conjectures of a Guilty Bystander?* 'Karl Barth had a dream about Mozart.' I found myself speculating, in December 1968, about conversations that might be going on in some heavenly waiting room between Merton and Barth. Apparently such very diverse figures: the greatest Protestant thinker of the twentieth century, and one of the most widely-publicized and widely-read Catholic writers of the age. What would they have to say to each other? Well of course, *Conjectures of a Guilty Bystander* begins to give you the answer to that. The conversation did not begin in the anteroom of heaven (or some department of purgatory) in 1968: it had begun several years earlier. 16 September 1960 is the first reference in Merton's journals to his reading of Karl Barth, and during the early '60s Barth was so much of a conversation partner for Merton in his private journal writing, that *Conjectures* itself is, for a long time, referred to in the journals under the provisional title *Barth's Dream* (which is still the title of the first part of the published journal, *Conjectures*).

'Karl Barth had a dream about Mozart,' and Merton was very deeply struck by what Barth had to say about Mozart. Mozart, according to Barth, posed a major theological problem: Barth's dream was about trying to get Mozart to explain to him why he was an unreconstructed (and not terribly devout) Roman Catholic. Barth took these things seriously and really wanted to know; but, Mozart had no answer to give him. Mozart had said all he wanted to say: and he hadn't said it in theological words. Mozart, said Barth, is

71

the 'divine child' in all of us. Merton seizes on this image, and says that, even for a committed Protestant theologian like Barth, it's the 'divine child,' the Mozart, who saves us.

> Barth says … 'It is a child, even a "divine" child, who speaks in Mozart's music to us.' Some…considered Mozart always a child in practical affairs. …At the same time Mozart, the child prodigy, 'was never allowed to be a child in the literal meaning of that word.' He gave his first concert at the age of six. Yet he was always a child 'in the higher meaning of that word.'
>
> Fear not, Karl Barth! [Merton continues]. Trust in the divine mercy. Though you have grown up to become a theologian, Christ remains a child in you. Your books (and mine) matter less than we might think: there is in us a Mozart who will be our salvation.[2]

But Merton connects this in his journals with a much deeper ground-swell of interest at that time in what he refers to as 'the *sophianic*': that is, that level of the world where divine wisdom in its receptive femininity is at work. That depth of silent receptivity, represented in scripture and tradition by the language of holy wisdom (particularly represented in the eastern Orthodox tradition by the icons of holy wisdom), is, for Merton, what Barth is feeling for—and not quite articulating. The 'divine child' belongs with this apprehension of divine *Sophia*, the wisdom at the heart of things. And Merton tends to read Barth at this point as if Barth the theologian stands simply for the principle of active—almost aggressive—divine love over against any attempt at human self-justification or human action. He fits Barth very neatly into the polarity between *agape* and *eros*: *agape* the divine love coming down actively, and *eros*, the hope-less, human attempt by desire and longing to rise to God, always frustrated. Barth the theologian is on the side of *agape* and yet (says Merton) scratch Barth a little and you'll find Mozart, you'll find *eros*; you'll find the divine yearning mediated through the human.

And that goes with Merton's reading of Barth at this point as someone advocating an extreme hostility to, or suspicion of, human culture, and also as someone privileging the cerebral over the emo-tional or imaginative. That is of course how Barth has often been read: but I want to suggest that Merton's reading of Barth moved on a good deal from that point, and moved on in such a way as to be of one piece with his apprehension of—and his use of—the very different religious world of Buddhism in his Christian journey. So that the bold suggestion I'm making is that Barth helped Merton to read Buddhists (though Barth, I suspect, would not have thanked me for this).

Even the very first quotation that Merton makes from Barth ought to flash a few warning signs: because that first quotation is from a Christmas sermon of Barth's in which Barth attacks the whole idea of religious system and religious proof. In other words Barth is undercutting his own intellectualism and cerebral temptation. Thus the Barth that Merton is reading is already rather more complex than simply the prophet of divine, aggressive, active *agape* mediated through the theologian's intellect, and yet secretly subverted by the divine child. And it's fascinating to trace in the journals of the early 1960s just how Merton's reading gradually opens out onto some deeper dimensions of Karl Barth.

In *Conjectures* later on, he is still reading Barth as someone wary of or hostile towards human culture, and compares him unfavourably both with Christopher Dawson (a great Roman Catholic social thinker) and with Dietrich Bonhoeffer; saying that Bonhoeffer stands much closer to Catholicism than Barth does. But that first layer of the Barth/Merton conversation is already beginning to give way in the journals of this period. Merton read Barth more and more deeply; and by 1963 he had begun to hear another music in him. Before '63 he had read little beyond one or two sermons and some slightly more journalistic pieces by Barth; but in '63, he was reading Barth's little book *Dogmatics in Outline*[3]—the lectures that Barth gave after the war in the ruins of Bonn University, which are certainly still the best short guide to Barth's thinking. If we turn to the journals of 1963–5 (represented especially in volume five, *Dancing in the Water of Life*) we see something new opening up. Merton has begun to understand that Barth's concept of God, Christ, and of faith is a concept far more in tune with some of his own deepest intuitions than he had ever spotted before. Here is some of what he wrote in the journal:

30 September 1963
A magnificent line from Karl Barth. 'Everyone who has to contend with unbelief should be advised that he ought not to take his own unbelief too seriously. Only faith is to be

taken seriously, and if we have faith as a grain of mustard seed, that suffices for the devil to have lost his game.' What stupendous implications in that![4]

Barth, in *Dogmatics in Outline,* is not simply mounting a conventional attack of *agape* against *eros,* faith against culture: he is rather saying that the self before God is not *serious,* it is *groundless.* It is not something that exists in its own density and solidity: the self before God is poised on the divine word, the divine communication, over an unfathomable abyss. It is both deadly serious in one sense, and totally unserious in another. It is not surprising that Merton returns several times in his journal entries to Barth's *humour* in *Dogmatics in Outline.* (It has to be said, against popular myth, that Barth can be a very funny writer indeed, and often is, in these lectures.) Merton (as we have noted already) picks up with delight the way in which Barth can use vivid imagery: 'Pontius Pilate creeps into the Creed like a dog into a tidy room'!

Now there are elements of the old typology still at work in Merton's reception of Barth at this time—as in the contrast that he draws between Barth and Frithjof Schuon (1907–98) at one point, as representing revelation over against a perennial philosophy of 'the religions.' Yet more and more, Merton is drawn into what seems to be the heart of Barth's theological vision, and finds there both a deep resonance and a profound challenge. The key passage comes in an entry for 24 October 1963: here it is in its original form from the journal, though a version of it is reproduced in *Conjectures,* crucially placed almost at the end of the book—as if it's a point towards which Merton is working. Merton opens with a quote from Barth:

> *24 October 1963*
> 'To be a man means to be situated in God's presence as Jesus is, that is, to be a bearer of the wrath of God.' ... We need the shock of this sentence—which is of course immediately qualified by Barth himself. And the qualification is implicit, for Jesus bears that wrath and lives. But the wrath is on us!
>
> And the Calvinist catechism: 'What understandest thou by the little word "suffered"?' 'That He all the time of His life, but especially at the end thereof, hath borne in body and soul the wrath of God against the whole human race.' How powerful, and how serious!

Catholic piety sees Christ suffering all His life, but in a different perspective. He is the bearer of all kinds of pains, but they are so to speak the pains of a person who has not been 'struck,' who is not under the wrath. They are quantitative, detailed, exquisite, etc. But the full enormity of sin is perhaps not seen as well as here, for God seems to be pleased with this pain. No! It is His wrath!

And Barth's terrific chapter on Pilate. I think I shall have to become a Christian.[5]

Merton deals here with one of the most difficult, challenging, unattractive, and indispensable bits of Barth—humanity under the wrath of God; *Jesus* under the wrath of God, in what Merton calls later an *ontological* sense of wrath—that is, the wrath of God as something written into *being* itself. Merton reads this as saying that God is not 'pleased' with who and what we have made ourselves. But therefore he is not *pleased* with suffering, either Christ's or ours, suffering as quantitively piled up in order to placate God. Understanding suffering as something we can 'store up' in order to make God be 'soft' on us is to misunderstand completely the nature of the wrath of God and the pain of Christ.

'I think I shall have to become a Christian,' says Merton, meaning, if I read him correctly, 'I think I shall have to understand that a proper theology of the death of Christ tells me I'm not *serious*.'[6] God is serious; my *condition* is serious; sin is serious; the Cross is serious. But somehow, out of all this comes the miracle, the 'unbearable lightness of being,' as you might say: the recognition that my reality rests 'like a feather on the breath of God.' It *is* because God speaks, because God loves, and it *is* for no other reason. And if we want to know what it *is* to say that I *am*, the only answer is, 'I *am* because of the love of God.' And when I seek to justify, defend or systematize what I am, I become 'serious.' I cease to be a feather on the breath of God and gravity draws me down into darkness.

This builds on Barth's quite complicated discussion of St Anselm as summarized by Merton in *Dancing in the Water of Life*,[7] where Merton moves through a conventional reading of St Anselm to emerge with a powerful conviction of the *point* of celebrating the death of Christ as celebrating the love of God, not celebrating the persuasive power of suffering. But that would take us even further afield, and Merton on Anselm would be another chapter or more. The important thing is that, at this particular stage, what Merton is picking up is Barth's sense of God's *freedom*. God freely causes us to be involved in the life of the Spirit by freely choosing the means of salvation, not being coerced, he says, by some eternal and impersonal decree. God freely chooses to bring about salvation through poverty and death: through a renunciation which makes room for the freedom of God. We read later on in *Dancing in the Water of Life*: 'In sacrificing the desire to be absent, man reveals the world to itself as the place of man's meeting with the glory of God in freedom.'[8] Although a summary of Merton's own reflections at that point, it might equally well be a summary of the first chapter of Barth's *Dogmatics in Outline*, which speaks very powerfully of the world—and the human world— as the theatre of God's glory and liberty.

Merton has absorbed in all this some of the most difficult and apparently unattractive elements of Barth, the interpreter of Calvin. He has understood that when Barth writes about the wrath of God, he is not writing about some emotional feeling that God has towards us which we have to calm down. He is talking rather about that wholly destructive order of being which we set up when we attempt to fill the space that should be filled by the freedom of the love of God. You can see how this is developed still further in more depth in some of the later journal entries. It's a very paradoxical kind of 'natural theology'; and much later on in *Dancing* (the entry for 12 August 1965[9]), Merton explains what he means—implicitly contrasting Barth here with 'the Barthians,' Barth's rather less gifted interpreters.

> *12 August 1965*
> Our very creation itself is a beginning of revelation. Making us in His image, God reveals Himself to us, we are already his words to ourselves! Our very creation itself is a vocation to union with Him and our life, and in the world around us, if we persist in honesty and simplicity, cannot help speaking of him and of our calling. But the trouble is that there are no 'pure' natural traditions and everything gets overlaid with error. Still, there is truth there for those who are still able to seek it, even if they are few. Ought it to be called 'theology'? That is a technical question.[10]

Our very creation is a vocation: once again the centrality in Barth's theology of the calling of God as the essence of the creative act is used by Merton to establish what he thinks is a kind of natural theology which avoids the reproach of simply trying to climb from the world to God by a ladder of analogy. Existence itself is a *word*, my being is God's *word* to me. And in that entry, Merton sees this as something quite in tune, not only with Barth, but with Anselm.

It's not that there is, from this perspective, something in us, some element of human longing, human *eros*, which links us to God and leads us to God: not that there's some bit of us which if we spot it correctly gives us the right clues to work out the existence of God. It's the bare fact of our *being*, resting on God's gift: that is, a 'word,' a calling, a summons, the beginning of union. And that is why I used earlier on the admittedly quite controversial word 'groundlessness.' I used it because it is one of the concepts that bridges something of the world of Barth and the world that Merton at the very same time was immersing himself in, more and more deeply: the world of Buddhist meditation and speculation. Groundlessness: there is no solid self independent of the relations, the chains of interaction, that compose the world; there is no solid self which exists over against God. There is only the call of God and the echo set up in creation: the possibility of union.

It is not to say everything is contained within God (this is not pantheism): it is to say rather that what *is,* is because God addresses it, because God relates to it. Although Merton doesn't seem to make the connection explicitly, this (as we saw in an earlier chapter) has all kinds of resonances with the Eastern Christian idea that it is the *logoi*, the words of God, which are the foundation of everything. Every reality is a communication of God, and everything exists therefore in virtue of God's communicating act.

Elements of Barth are feeding in here to the way in which Merton in this period is appropriating Taoism and Zen particularly; they become part of his own revolt against the seriousness of images of the self.

18 June 1965
'Solitude' becomes for me less and less of a specialty, and simply 'life' itself. I do not seek to 'be a solitary' or anything else, for 'being anything' is a distraction. It is enough to be, in an ordinary human mode, with only hunger and sleep, one's cold and warmth; rising and going to bed. Putting on blankets and taking them off (two last night—it is

cold for June!) Making coffee and then drinking it. Defrost-
ing the refrigerator, reading, meditating, working (ought to
get on to the article on symbolism today), praying. I live
as my fathers have lived on this earth until eventually I die.
Amen. There is no need to make an assertion of my life,
especially to assert it as MINE, though it is doubtless not
somebody else's.[11]

28 August 1965
    I realized then that I have been running the risk, these
past few days, of tying myself down with a mental delu-
sion—taking the hermitage too seriously and myself with
it—identifying myself with this stupid little cottage as if
my whole life was bound up with it. What total absurdity! Looking at the hills and recovering the freedom of true
prayer (of which, incidentally I have had so much in the
hermitage too), I realized, that what is important is not the
house, not the hermit image, but my own self and my son-
ship as a child of God.[12]

Merton is in revolt against the *seriousness* of the self-image, and
therefore, with an extraordinary prescience and depth, sketching out
what is involved in an acceptance of what he calls an 'unavoidable
wrongness'[13] in us.

5 July 1965
    Certainly enough is evident merely in this Journal to de-
stroy me for ever after I am dead. But that is the point: not
to live as one who can be so 'destroyed.' This means not in-
geniously discovering infallible ways of being 'true' in the
eyes of others and of posterity (if any!) but of accepting my
untruth in the untransferrable anguish that is characteristic
of death and leaving all 'justification' to God. Everything
else is only wrath, flame, torment, and judgement.[14]

I think you can see in that extract what Merton has done with Barth's
notion of the wrath of God. 'Wrath' is what happens when we take
ourselves seriously, when the self-image takes over from reality.
And that passage is to me a very poignant 'opening out' onto the
agonies of introspection in *Learning to Love* (the sixth volume of
the journals), the volume which covers those anguished months of

Merton's love affair. Here I can only refer to a few typical state-
ments, where all of that thinking and reflecting of a couple of years
previously comes into focus in the light of an experience of *wrongness*; being at odds, being unable to provide a self-justification and
unable to settle down with a satisfying image of the self. As Merton
says—rather poignantly and wryly—in the journals, he is both a bad
monk and a bad lover. There is no way of bringing it all together in a
single frame. So he can write—in a way markedly contrasting with
some of what he said earlier about Christopher Dawson—about the
risks of an escape into a 'beautiful lost world of extinct Christian
culture. Will that simply reinforce the deceptions and delusions of
my "monastic" life? I don't say these are answers: but they are real
questions.'

> *5 September 1966*
> What I see is this: that while I imagine I was function-
> ing fairly successfully, I was living a sort of patched up,
> crazy existence, a series of rather hopeless improvisations,
> a life of unreality in many ways. Always underlain by a
> certain solid silence and presence, a faith, a clinging to the
> invisible God—and this clinging (perhaps rather His hold-
> ing on to me) has been in the end the only thing that made
> sense. The rest has been absurdity. ... There is 'I'—this
> patchwork, this bundle of questions and doubts and obses-
> sions, this gravitation to silence and to the woods and to
> love. This incoherence!!
> There is no longer anything to pride myself in, least
> of all 'being a monk' or being anything—a writer or any-
> thing.[15]

Again, that same month.

> Where I am now, nothing unambiguous is possible. In a
> certain sense *I have to be wrong* up to a point, and what I am
> trying to learn is how to be at least simple and honest about
> it, and not try to say I am right, and not try to whitewash
> myself in terms of something or someone I cannot be. I am
> neither a good monk nor a good lover.[16]

In those pages some of what both Barth and Buddhism have fed
into Merton becomes incarnate in the most uncomfortable and challenging way. Because if it's true that I am a 'feather on the breath

of God,' that I exist because called, summoned into relation by God, that I have no seriousness within myself, but only the joyful 'unbearable lightness' of knowing myself held by God—if this is true, then there is never going to be a way in which I can map my life, my sense of my identity onto a fore-ordained pattern of *rightness* and justification. I am bound to be dependent. I am bound to be receiving. I am bound to put on hold the issue of whether I can show myself to be 'right.' And it leads Merton to make some very stinging remarks in these journals about 'religion' as a means of self-justification, religion as a drama which seeks to gloss or to soften the challenge of faith: a very Barthian theme indeed. There's another telling little aside where Merton is reflecting on Teilhard de Chardin. He was initially quite enthusiastic about Teilhard, then read a bit and found it much duller than he expected.

10 June 1967
    Are the neologisms of Teilhard much better? Good intentions, heart in the right place, wanting the right thing, but did he really have the necessary gifts? If it comes to science I would gladly read later and better scientists. If it comes to poets ... he does not even begin to be one. As for theology, I must admit that I become more and more suspicious of it in its contemporary form. After Barth.[17] ...

As if something about the ambitious, harmonic cosmology of Teilhard comes to be insupportable once you've really digested Barth not only as a theologian, but as someone describing your reality, your *unjustifiable* reality which depends on the mercy of God. I am not saying that we should fully endorse that judgement of Teilhard: it's a very typical bit of Merton's wild over-statement. But the little, uncompleted sentence, 'After Barth.' is very significant there.
    He sums up a lot of this in an entry from the private journal written in the summer of 1966 and designed for the woman he loved.

20 June 1966
    The great joke is this: having a self that is to be taken seriously, that is to be proved, free, right, logical, consistent, beautiful, successful, and in a word 'not absurd.'

4 February 1967
    Let the idol fall on its face in the presence of the hidden child.[18]

This brings us back to where we started—only the 'divine child' this time is not a sort of innocent, sophianic, indwelling reality, yearning heavenwards towards God; or a sort of buried innocence that you can strip your way down to. The divine child this time is the birth of God's freedom in the emptiness of solitude and the emptiness of realizing that there is no justification. And even having said that, we have to be careful: the full quotation is: 'Let the idol fall on its face in the presence of the hidden child. (Yeah, but beware.)'

We come again full-circle to Barth and Mozart. The experience of real *eros* in 1966 was not for Merton a revelation of original innocence or of a deeply buried 'image,' but a revelation of the groundlessness of the self, a revelation of the inescapability of finding yourself wrong—and neither justifying the wrong nor pretending to be justified in any other way: a revelation of groundlessness (and yes, in that sense, 'Buddhist' up to a point), but still underpinned by an essentially Christ-focused awareness, awareness of the bearing of 'wrath' in Christ. It is Christ, in life and death and resurrection, who shows us how *unserious* we are, how little we can begin to do to justify ourselves, because everything is gift. And it may sound strange to read incarnation and cross and resurrection in that light, and yet in all those millions of words of Barth's *Church Dogmatics*, that is where he is driving. Although Merton had not worked his way through those millions of words, he *had* apprehended something central and focal in Barth's vision: we are not 'pleasing' to God; yet God wills to be pleased. That is to say that we are not condemned to keep God happy, we are not bound to the fiery wheel of entertaining God, placating God or preserving God's good moods. Because God's pleasure is God's being and God's will directed towards us in creation and redemption, and therefore all we can do is say 'yes' to it. To know this is to be finally free from the idols of the self.

Merton didn't discover all this in Barth; it is already strongly adumbrated in the 1950s in parts of *Thoughts in Solitude*—one of his most profound and abidingly impressive books. But somehow making the Christological connection seems to be one of those things that, with all the intellectual and spiritual and emotional turbulence of the mid-1960s in Merton's life, anchored him in the classical Christian vision of the Son sent forth from the Father, returning to the Father ('the Son's journey into the far country,' as Barth calls it), with the whole of our life, our universe, our individual pilgrimage, swept up into that movement of outgoing and returning love, a love bestowed, a love which is also our homecoming, a love so profoundly anchored ontologically in the reality of God, eternally, non-negotiably, that the only thing we can do about any attempt on our part to think that we have a constructive or determining role in this is to laugh. Barth's unseriousness, Merton's unseriousness, and perhaps Mozart's glorious unseriousness all converge here. To say this is not to minimize the depth of human betrayal or the intensity of human suffering. But it *is* to say (to go back to that phrase of Merton's in the '66/'67 journals), that 'the great joke is having a self that is to be taken seriously,' when what is to be taken seriously— and yet unbearably lightly—is only and eternally God.

Thomas Merton: summer 1966

The Old Choir at the Abbey of Gethsemani

Thomas Merton: summer 1966[1]

Bright post-examination weather; in the redundant
classroom, the only point seems here, the belly
of Kentucky heat, the shaven sweating mariners
singing Gregorian shanties in a slow
light evening. What do I want? What sixteen-year-olds want,
no doubt; but also: to learn how to sail that sweaty ship,
words falling moistly from the timber, shining,
Latin, American, French. And the horizon that you think
(so slow the light, so slow the gestures and the voices)
night never quite closes on.

                The same month
you made a landfall, emptied on to the shore,
gasping and heaving against a new hard element,
against the solid sand. And now I read you, years on,
leap and flail, mouth wide, reaching—you once-fluent fellow—
for the words to fix it, finding in the unfixable
a bizarre homeliness. You spent my sixteenth birthday
making a clean(ish) breast of things to the steel smile
of Abbot James. You staged show after show
for friends, then cancelled. Not to make sense is
what most matters.

                What was I seeing,
then, that summer? light from a dead star?
Not quite. But who could tell the night, closing its mouth,
the hard sand, were, after all, where the hot songs
would lead? Practise the Gothic scales for long enough
and they will conjure, surprisingly, this place, flat concrete
    blocks,
convenience foods, an empty page to look into,
finding the anger; painting, then blotting faces you might
    wear,
hers, yours, that only in fiction would stand still.
Not to make sense, inside the keel of sweating ribs,
not to make sense but room.

Afterword

Rabbi Bunam said to his disciples: 'Everyone must have two pockets, so that he can reach into the one or the other, according to his needs. In his right pocket are to be the words: "For my sake the world was created," and in his left: "I am earth and ashes."'

Martin Buber, Tales of the Hasidim

Reading these *Engagements with Thomas Merton*, I am impressed by what Archbishop Rowan calls 'the human complexity of the man,' the 'chameleon-like dimension to his mind.' I take to heart what Rowan says in the poem that forms his conclusion: 'Not to make sense is what most matters.' Yet at the same time I find in these chapters certain connecting threads that confer upon the present book an underlying unity. And among these threads the most important for me is Merton's understanding of the human person. Here, I feel, is the one root under many branches.

Merton's understanding of personhood, however, is – like Merton himself – not only complex but in many ways paradoxical. For Merton, as for Pascal, the human being is at one and the same time both 'all' and 'nothing.' We are, in the words of St Gregory of Nazianzus, 'earthly yet heavenly . . . midway between majesty and lowliness.' Merton is acutely aware of both the pockets to which Rabbi Bunam refers.

'For my sake the world was created': Merton sets an exceedingly high value on our human nature. We are God's 'living image,' called to reach out to the Divine and the Eternal: in Merton's words, 'Our very creation itself is a vocation to union with Him.' Each of us is, as Rowan puts it, *homo liturgicus,* 'nature's Priest,' 'the vehicle of theophany in the world,' called to offer the world back to the Creator in thanksgiving.

Moreover, because God is free, we human beings in the Divine image are also free. His uncreated freedom is infinite; our created freedom is finite, yet it is none the less genuine. And, because we are free, each of us actualizes the Divine image within us in his or her distinctive and unrepeatable way. Merton speaks in powerful terms about the uniqueness of each human person. 'I have my own special peculiar destiny,' he writes, 'which no one else has or ever will have. . . . My own individual destiny is a meeting, an encounter with God that He has destined for me alone. His glory in me will be to receive from me something which he can never receive from anyone else.' In this way, each of us is a 'new word for God.' I am reminded here of two Jewish sayings recorded by Martin Buber: 'God never does the same thing twice,' and 'The world has need of every single person.'

Applying to the realm of time this notion of the uniqueness of each human person, Merton speaks also of the 'unique instant.' Our fallen experience of time often involves a sense of boredom and repetition. But the restoration of the Divine image within us brings about a discovery or recovery of the radiance of the present moment. Here, now, at this very instant, I come face to face with the *kairos*, the moment of opportunity. Here, now, I hold infinity in the palm of my hand and eternity in an hour.

This emphasis upon the uniqueness of each person, as Rowan recognizes, might lead to an unhealthy individualism. In fact Merton avoids this danger by insisting upon what Paul Evdokimov terms the 'collegiality' of the human person. 'The spirit of man,' says Rowan, applying this to Merton's standpoint, 'at its deepest level is "intentionally" towards the other'; and appositely he quotes Evdokimov: 'We can never keep ourselves alone before God; we are saved only together, "collegially," as Soloviev said: "he will be saved who saves others."' *Unus Christianus, nullus Christianus*, it was said in the early Church: one Christian, isolated, cut off from the total Body, is no true Christian. By the same token, it may be affirmed *Una persona, nulla persona*: one person, inward-looking, refusing to relate to others, is not a true person. We only become authentic persons when we are able to say with full conviction: I need you in order to be myself.

Merton makes use in this context of the distinction between individual and person. This is helpful, so long as it is not forgotten that in becoming a person-in-relation, I do not cease to be an individual. The individual/person contrast is one of those polarities in which the first term of the polarity – in this case, the individual – is not abolished but enhanced when taken up into the second term, the person. In all this I am reminded of what the Anglican poet-theologian Charles Williams called 'the apprehension of the Co-inherence,' 'the way of exchange,' and 'the practice of substituted love.' As he put it in one of his poems: 'dying each other's life, living each other's death.'

Thus far I have dwelt upon Merton's intensely positive estimate of human personhood, in all its uniqueness and interdependence: 'For my sake the world was created.' Yet he does not forget Rabbi Bunam's second pocket: 'I am earth and ashes.' In his thinking he assigns a central place to the theme of the 'illusory self'; this, says Rowan, is 'something utterly fundamental to Merton,' something indeed that brings him close to the Buddhist tradition So he speaks of himself in deprecating terms as 'this patchwork, this bundle of questions and doubts and obsessions, . . . This incoherence!! There is no longer anything to pride myself in, least of all "being a monk" or being anything – a writer or anything.' On another occasion he asserts, 'We must long to learn the secret of our own nothingness.' We should not take ourselves too seriously.

Yet that is not Merton's last word. In the words of Archbishop Rowan: 'Somehow, out of all of this comes the miracle, the "unbearable lightness of being," as you might say: the recognition that my reality rests "like a feather on the breath of God."' In myself I may be a 'patchwork,' an 'incoherence,' a 'nothing'; yet in God I have eternal and inexhaustible meaning. 'I *am* because of the love of God.'

Such is the paradox, the strange antinomy, in the Christian vision of human personhood: 'nothing' and yet 'all.' For Merton, as for the Greek Fathers, however rigorously we seek to analyse our personhood, in the end it eludes our grasp. In the words once more of Evdokimov, quoted by Rowan, 'The *Deus absconditus*, the mysterious God, has created His counterpart: the *homo absconditus*, the mysterious man, His living image.' Counterbalancing our negative theology, we need to uphold a negative anthropology. 'Who is it that can tell me who I am?' The answer to King Lear's anguished cry is by no means simple and obvious. We do not properly understand what is involved in being a person, what are the possibilities as yet latent in our human personalness, what is the ultimate fulfilment of being a person.

'The greatest of all lessons is to know yourself,' says Clement of Alexandria. 'For if someone knows himself, he will know God; and if he knows God, he will become like God.' Yet this 'greatest of all lessons,' as Thomas Merton readily acknowledges, is not easily learnt. In the words of the German Romantic poet Novalis, 'The deepest secret is man himself.'

Metropolitan Kallistos Ware of Diokleia
Ecumenical Patriarchate

Notes

Chapter 1 'A person that nobody knows'

1. Thomas Merton: *The Sign of Jonas* (New York: Harcourt Brace, 1953), p.246 [R/1981, Orlando, FL: Harcourt, 1981]
2. *2 Corinthians* 6:9
3. *The Asian Journal of Thomas Merton* (New York: New Directions, 1973), pp.287–8 [R/, New York: New Directions, 1978]
4. *Ibid*, p.286
5. Thomas Merton: *The Climate of Monastic Prayer* (Dublin: Irish UP, 1969; Collegeville, MA: Cistercian Publications, 1973), p.37
6. *Sign of Jonas*, p.187

Chapter 2 'Bread in the Wilderness'

1. *Conjectures of A Guilty Bystander* (London: Burns and Oates, 1968), pp.308–10
2. In his Foreword to *Elected Silence* (the British edition of *The Seven Storey Mountain)*
3. See, for example, *Climate of Monastic Prayer,* note to page 116.
4. *Conjectures,* page 309. Cf. Paul Evdokimov: *The Struggle with God* (Paramus, NJ: Paulist-Newman Press, 1966), pages 99–105
5. Thomas Merton: *A Secular Journal* (New York: Farrar, Straus & Cudahy, 1959), pp.77–9, 79–80, 84–88
6. *Ibid*, p.80
7. *Ibid*, pp.68–71
8. *Elected Silence,* p.215
9. *Ibid,* p.216
10. Paul Evdokimov: *L'Orthodoxie (*Neuchâtel: Delachaux and Niestle, 1959), p.20
11. *Struggle with God*, p.93
12. *Ibid,* p.113
13. Fyodor Dostoevsky: *The Brothers Karamazov*, bk II, ch 5 (I quote from David Magarshack's translation in the Penguin Classics, vol 1, p.69)
14. See *Struggle with God*, chapter 1, *passim*
15. *L'Orthodoxie,* p.98
16. *Struggle with God,* p.104
17. *Climate of Monastic Prayer,* p.37; my italics.
18. *Struggle with God*, pp.117–18.
19. *Karamazov*, bk V, ch 5; Penguin edition, vol 1, pp.288–311
20. *Struggle with God,* p.118

21. *Karamazov,* Penguin edition, vol 1, pp.295

22. *Struggle with God,* p.120

23. *Ibid,* p.122

24. *Ibid,* p.123

25. Again a theme found in Dostoyevsky; see, for example, *The Devils,* pt I, ch 4 (Penguin edition, page 154), 'The Mother of God is a great mother earth.'

26. Patrologia Graeca 65:363; 564; quoted in *The Struggle with God,* p.128

27. Patrologia Graeca 65:224; quoted in *ibid,* p.128

28. *Ibid,* page 129

29. Thomas Merton: *Contemplation in a World of Action,* Gethsemani Studies in Psychological and Religious Anthropology (Notre Dame, IN: U of Notre Dame Press, 1998, R/2001), pp.284–5 (in the essay on 'The Spiritual Father in the Desert Tradition')

30. See particularly *Climate of Monastic Prayer,* p.37

31. *Sign of Jonas,* p.246

32. *Climate of Monastic Prayer,* p.39; cf. 'The Identity Crisis,' in *Contemplation in a World of Action,* pp.56–82.

33. *Raids on the Unspeakable* (New York: New Directions, 1966), p.19

34. *Struggle with God,* p.105

35. *Ibid,* p.104 (note that the expression 'transformation of consciousness' is the title of a chapter in J. Higgins: *Merton's Theology of Prayer,* Cistercian Studies, 18 [Spencer, MA: Cistercian Publications, 1971])

36. *Ibid,* p.130: the concept of *epiclesis* is very important in Evdokimov's thought on a variety of subjects, especially liturgy and iconography.

37. See the essays 'Contemplation in a World of Action' and 'Is the Contemplative Life Finished?' in *Contemplation in a World of Action*; and cf. chapter 3 in Higgins, op. cit.

38. *Contemplation in a World of Action,* p.340 (cf. pp.205–17)

39. *The New Man* (New York: Farrar, Straus and Cudahy, 1961), p.34

40. *Ibid,* p.149

41. *Secular Journal,* p.98

42. *La connaissance de Dieu selon Ia tradition orientale,* page 11 *(*cf. *The Struggle with God,* page 2); this is well said, but it is only fair to add that, as an exegesis of *I Peter* 3:4, it is somewhat fanciful.

43. See especially *L 'Orthodoxie,* pp.68–72, cf, Vladimir Lossky, *The Mystical Theology of the Eastern Church,* chapter 6.

44. See, for example, *Struggle with God,* pp.63–4; *La connaissance de Dieu,* p.32.

45. See *L 'Orthodoxie,* pp.312ff

46. *The Struggle with God,* p.137

47. *Ibid*, pp.167, 194

48. See *Struggle with God*, pt II, especially chs 3 and 4.

49. *Disputed Questions*, p.188

50. *Sign of Jonas*, pp.186–88

51. *Ibid*, p.186

52. *Ibid*, p.187

53. *Ibid*, p.187

54. *Ibid*, pp.196–97

55. *Secular Journal*, pp.186–87

56. *Ibid*, p.187

57. *Struggle with God*, p.198 (cf. *L'Orthodoxie*, p.165).

58. *Ibid*, p.208

59. See Augustine, *De civitate Dei, 1.* 20, c. 70: 'Omnes sacerdotes, quoniam membra sunt unius sacerdotis.'

60. *Struggle with God*, p.200.

61. *L'art de l'icône*, p.43.

62. For the best exposition in English of Maximus' thought, see Lars Thunberg: *Microcosm and Mediator: the Theological Anthropology of Maximus the Confessor* (Peru, IL: Open Court, 1995)

63. Thomas Merton: *Bread in the Wilderness* (Collegeville, MN: Liturgical Press, 1953), p.51

64. *Disputed Questions*, pp.3–67

65. *Ibid*, p.18

66. *Ibid*, p.49

67. *Contemplation in a World of Action*, page 188

68. *Ibid*, p.189

69. *Ibid*, p.189; my italics

70. *Ibid*, p.189

71. *Ibid*, p.189

72. *Conjectures*, p.200

73. See the essays on 'Sacred Art and the Spiritual Life' and 'Absurdity in Sacred Decoration' in *Disputed Questions*.

74. See, for example, *La connaissance de Dieu*, chapter 8; *L 'art de l'icône*, pt I, ch 7, and *L'Orthodoxie*, pp.220, 229

75. *Disputed Questions*, p.155

76. *Ibid*, p.154

77. *Raids on the Unspeakable*, pages 155–161

78. *Ibid*, p.157

79. *Ibid*, p.158, my italics

80. *Ibid*, pp.165–175

81. *Ibid*, p.166

82. *Ibid*, p.167, my italics

83. *Ibid,* p.168

84. *Ibid,* p.173

85. *Contemplation in a World of Action,* p.188

86. See above, n.44

87. See, for example, 'The Power and Meaning of Love' *(Disputed Questions,* pp.97–126); *The New Man,* pages 64f, 106, 115; *Life and Holiness* (New York: Herder and Herder, 1963), p.112; and cf. the passage in *The Waters of Siloe* (New York: Harcourt, Brace, 1949) pages 276–282 on the different kinds of 'solitude,' permissible and impermissible, in the cenobitic life.

88. Struggle with God, p.113

Chapter 3 'New Words for God'

1. Thomas Merton: *Raids on The Unspeakable* (Tunbridge Wells, Kent: Burns & Oates, 1977) pp.118–124

2. *Raids*, pp.125–135

3. *Raids*, p.132

4. W. H. Auden: 'August 1968,' *Collected Poems (*London: Faber & Faber, 1976), p.604

5. *Raids*, pp.122–3

6. Letter to Mark van Doren, 30 March 1948 in Thomas Merton: *The Road to Joy: Letters to New and Old Friends*, selected and ed.: Robert E. Daggy (New York: Farrar, Straus & Giroux, 1989), p.22

7. *Raids*, p.133

8. *Ibid*, p.124

9. Letter to Sister Therese Lentfoehr, 18 Nov 1948: *Road to Joy,* p.189

10. W. H. Auden: 'Dichtung und Wahrheit,' *Collected Poems*, p.643

11. *The Ascent of Mount Carmel*, bk II c. vi

12. Letter to Mark van Doren: *Road to Joy,* p.22

Chapter 4 'The Only Real City'

1. *Secular Journal*, p.91

2. Michael Mott: *The Seven Mountains of Thomas Merton* (Boston: Houghton Miffline, 1984), p.396

3. See Elisabeth Young-Bruehl, *Hannah Arendt: For Love of the World* (New Haven and London: Yale UP, 1982), pp.318–22; and George Kateb: *Hannah Arendt: Politics, Conscience, Evil* (Oxford: Martin Robertson, 1984), pp.3–14

4. Thomas Merton: *Turning Towards the World: The Pivotal Years (1960–1963)*, The Journals of Thomas Merton, vol. 4 (Harper: San Francisco, 1996), pp.5–6

5. *Ibid*, pp.11–13

6. *Ibid*, pp.11

7. *Ibid*, pp.12–13

8. *Secular Journal*, p.94

9. *Ibid*, p.93

10. *Turning Towards the World*, p.12

11. *Ibid*, pp.138–9

12. *Ibid*, p.34

13. e.g., *ibid*, pp.65, 88, 171, 222

14. *Ibid*, p.150

15. *Ibid*, pp.150–1

16. c.f., *ibid*, pp.76–7

17. *Conjectures*, p.288

18. *Ibid*, p.176

19. *Turning Towards the World*, p.107

20. *Ibid*, p.157

21. *Ibid*, p.222

22. *Ibid*, pp.202–3

23. *Ibid*, p.201

24. *Ibid*, p.206

25. *Ibid*, p.202

26. *Ibid*, p.211

27. *Ibid*, p.206

28. *Ibid*, pp.238–9

29. *Ibid*, p.176

30. *Ibid*, p.239

31. 'A City is Something You Do ...' in Paul Pearson, ed.: *Thomas Merton: A Mind Awake in the Dark* (Abergavenny, 2002), pp.130–140

32. *Ibid*, p.138

33. *Turning Towards the World*, pp.49–50

34. Oliver Clément: *Transfigurer le temps: notes sur le temps à la lumière de la tradition orthodoxe* (Neuchâtel/Paris, Delachaux et Niestlé, 1959)

35. Thomas Merton: *A Search for Solitude: Pursuing the Monk's True Life (1952–1960)*, The Journals of Thomas Merton, vol. 3 (Harper: San Francisco, 1996), pp.85–6

36. Thomas Merton: *Witness to Freedom: Letters in Times of Crisis* (New York: Farrer, Strause, Giroux, 1994), pp.4–6

37. See especially *Turning Towards the World, pp.39–42*

38. Clément: *Transfigurer,* p.207; translation by the present author

39. *Conjectures*, p.308

40. *Turning Towards the World*, p.349

41. *Conjectures*, p.309

42. *Ibid,* p.310

43. See, for example, *Turning Towards the World*, p.138

44. *Ibid*, p.160

45. e.g., pp.87–88, 144

46. *Conjectures*, p.265

47. *Turning Towards the World*, p.310

48. Thomas Merton: *Dancing in the Water of Life: Seeking Peace in the Hermitage (1963–1965)*, The Journals of Thomas Merton, vol. 5 (Harper: San Francisco, 1997), pp.26–7; cf, *Conjectures*, pp.317–8)

49. *Ibid*, p.27

50. *Turning Towards the World*, p.21

Chapter 5 'Not Being Serious'

1. Prepared for a lecture given on 10 December 2008 to the UK Thomas Merton Society (at St Cyprian's, Clarence Gate, London) on the occasion of the fortieth anniversary of Merton's death in 1968. Karl Barth, the great Swiss Reformed theologian, died on the same day as Merton.

2. *Conjectures*, pp.3–4

3. Karl Barth's *Dogmatics in Outline*, Eng. trans., G T Thompson (London: SCM Press, 1949)

4. *Dancing in the Water of Life*, p.20

5. *Ibid*, pp.26–7

6. *Ibid*, p.27

7. *Ibid*, p.28–9

8. *Ibid*, p.73

9. *Ibid*, p.279

10. *Ibid*, p.279. Interestingly, this entry also includes a mention of Merton's contacts with Zen.

11. *Ibid*, p.257

12. *Ibid*, p.287

13. *Ibid*, p.265

14. *Ibid*, p.265

15. *Learning to Love*, p.125

16. *Ibid*, p.141

17. *Ibid*, pp.247–8

18. *Ibid*, pp.323, 358

Thomas Merton: summer 1966

1. At this time Merton was entangled in his tormenting and unconsummated love affair.